Using Accounting Software

Tutorial

Jacqui Barnard

Debbie Board

Published by Osborne Books Limited
Tel 01905 748071
Email books@osbornebooks.co.uk
Website www.osbornebooks.co.uk

Design by Laura Ingham

Printed by CPI Group (UK) Limited, Croydon, CR0 4YY, on environmentally friendly, acid-free paper from managed forests.

MIX
Paper from responsible sources
FSC® C019777

British Library Cataloguing in Publication Data
A catalogue record for this book is available from the British Library

ISBN 978 1909173 736

Contents

Introduction

Qualifications covered

This book has been written specifically to cover the Unit 'Using Accounting Software' which is mandatory for the following qualifications:

- AAT Foundation Certificate in Accounting – Level 2
- AAT Foundation Diploma in Accounting and Business – Level 2
- AAT Foundation Award in Accounting Software – Level 2
- AAT Foundation Certificate in Accounting at SCQF Level 5

The book contains clear and practical explanations of how to set up and run a desktop version of Sage. The Sage system (Version 22) has been chosen as it is widely used both by businesses and by training providers.

A Case Study – Tapper Timber – runs through the chapters. The Activities at the end of each chapter contain short questions to help consolidate learning and inputting tasks to develop Sage inputting skills. Answers to the short questions and printouts of the Sage input are included at the end of the book to enable students to check progress.

Osborne Study and Revision Materials

The materials featured on the previous page are tailored to the needs of students studying this unit and revising for the assessment. They include:

- **Workbooks:** paperback books with practice activities and exams
- **Student Zone:** access to Osborne Books online resources
- **Osborne Books App:** Osborne Books ebooks for mobiles and tablets

Visit www.osbornebooks.co.uk for details of study and revision resources and access to online material.

1 Introduction to using accounting software

this chapter covers...

■ The structure of an accounting software program is based on manual bookkeeping systems. It includes the Sales Ledger, Purchase Ledger, Cash Book and General Ledger.

■ Computers require input of data – which can either be carried out manually from sources such as financial documents or can be imported from other computer systems.

■ Computers also output data in the form of 'hard copy' printouts and electronic data which can be emailed or exported to other computer programs.

■ It is important to establish the principles of good housekeeping for computers. In other words, knowing how to look after the computer software and avoid losing the data held on it.

■ We will look at:

  – the use of passwords and access rights to the computer accounting system

  – logging onto the computer and dealing with dates

  – saving and backing up data

  – restoring data in Sage

  – software problems

INTRODUCTION TO ACCOUNTING SOFTWARE

a growth area

Although some organisations, particularly small businesses, still use paper-based accounting systems, most are now operating computerised accounting systems.

Small and medium-sized businesses can buy 'off-the-shelf' accounting programs from suppliers such as Sage while larger businesses may opt to have custom-designed programs. Computer accounting programs are easy to use and can automate operations which take much more time and effort in a manual system.

links with traditional bookkeeping

If you are studying bookkeeping or accounting, your study is likely to concentrate initially on paper-based systems. The reason for this is that when you use a paper-based system you have to do all the work manually and so you can understand the theory that underlies the system: you prepare the documents, make entries in the accounts, balance the cash book, and so on. You know where all the figures are entered, and why they are entered. If you know how a paper-based system works, you will be in a much better position to understand the operation of a computer-based system.

desktop or cloud?

Accounting software packages are available either in desktop form or in online (cloud-based) form.

Until recently accounting software programs were installed on desktop computers or local networks where the program and the data was maintained within the business computer system. Cloud-based accounting software programs now offer an alternative to in-house systems. They allow users such as colleagues or accountants to work from the same data at any time and from any location that has a computer with an internet connection. Data is securely backed up automatically as it is input.

FEATURES OF COMPUTER ACCOUNTING

facilities

A typical accounting software program will offer a number of facilities:

- on-screen input and printout of sales invoices and credit notes
- automatic updating of customer accounts with sales transactions

- recording of suppliers' invoices
- automatic updating of supplier accounts with details of purchases
- recording of money paid into bank or cash accounts
- recording of payments to suppliers and for expenses

management reports

An accounting software program can provide instant reports for management, for example:

- an aged debtors summary – showing who owes what and for what period of time
- activity reports on customer and supplier accounts
- activity reports on expenses accounts

advantages of an accounting software program

Computer accounting programs are popular because they offer a number of distinct advantages over paper-based systems:

- they save time and therefore money
- they tend to be more accurate because they rely on single-entry input (one amount per transaction) rather than double-entry bookkeeping
- they can provide the managers of the organisation with a clear and up-to-date picture of what is happening

computer accounting and ledgers

The 'ledgers' of a business are basically the books of the business. 'The ledgers' is a term used to describe the way the accounts of the business are grouped into different sections.

There are four main ledgers in a traditional accounting system:

- **sales ledger** contains the accounts of receivables (debtors), ie customers
- **purchases ledger** contains the accounts of payables (creditors), ie suppliers
- **cash book** contains the main cash book and the petty cash book
- **general ledger** (also called nominal or main ledger) contains the remaining accounts, eg expenses (including purchases), income (including sales), assets, loans, inventory (stock), VAT

A diagram illustrating these ledgers is shown on the next page. The structure of a computer accounting system is based on these ledgers. It may also include stock control and be linked to a payroll processing program.

The full range of modules within Sage (shown below) is accessed from the vertical toolbar or from the MODULES drop-down menu on the toolbar. The notes to the side explain what some of the modules are. Note that accounting software packages vary in levels of sophistication; you may be working with one that does not include product records or invoice printing.

Please note that the screens shown in these chapters may not necessarily be exactly the same as those on your computer because programs are regularly updated. This should not be a problem, however, because the basic principles of using the software are likely to remain exactly the same.

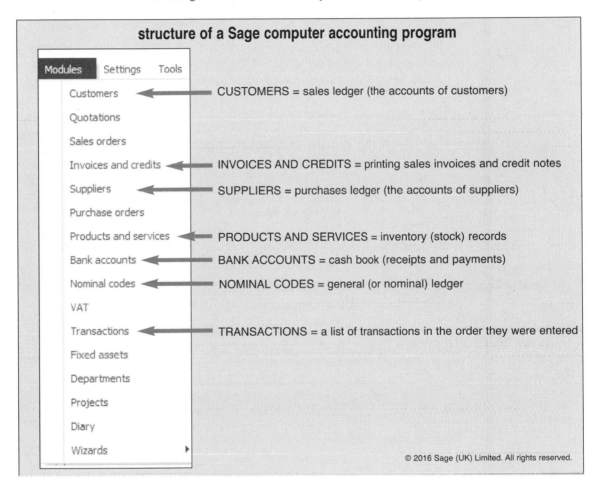

structure of a Sage computer accounting program

CUSTOMERS = sales ledger (the accounts of customers)

INVOICES AND CREDITS = printing sales invoices and credit notes

SUPPLIERS = purchases ledger (the accounts of suppliers)

PRODUCTS AND SERVICES = inventory (stock) records

BANK ACCOUNTS = cash book (receipts and payments)

NOMINAL CODES = general (or nominal) ledger

TRANSACTIONS = a list of transactions in the order they were entered

computerised ledgers – an integrated system

Before we look at the various functions, it is important to appreciate that a computerised ledger system is **fully integrated.** This means that when a business transaction is input on the computer it is normally recorded in two accounts at the same time, although only one amount is entered. Take the three transactions shown in the diagram on the next page:

- a business buys from a supplier on credit (ie the business gets the goods but will pay later)
- a business sells to a customer on credit (ie the business sells the goods but will receive payment later)
- a business pays an advertising bill

At the centre of an integrated program is the General Ledger which deals with all the accounts except customers' accounts and suppliers' accounts. It is affected one way or another by most transactions.

The diagram below shows how the three 'ledgers' link with the General Ledger. Note in each case how an account in the General Ledger is affected by each of the three transactions. This is the double-entry bookkeeping system at work. The advantage of the computer system is that in each case only one entry has to be made. Life is made a great deal simpler this way!

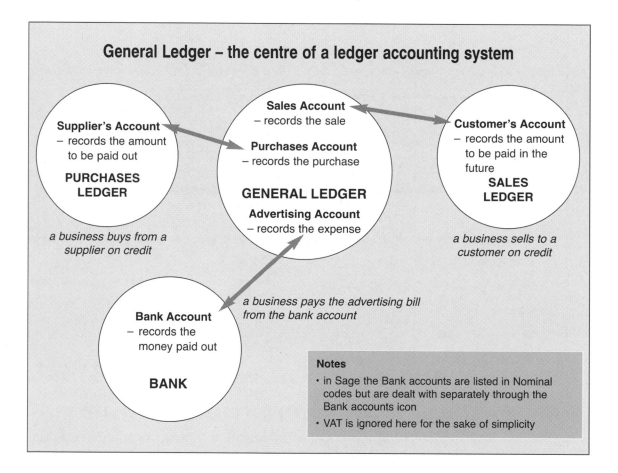

General Ledger – the centre of a ledger accounting system

Supplier's Account
– records the amount to be paid out
PURCHASES LEDGER

Sales Account
– records the sale
Purchases Account
– records the purchase
GENERAL LEDGER
Advertising Account
– records the expense

Customer's Account
– records the amount to be paid in the future
SALES LEDGER

a business buys from a supplier on credit

a business sells to a customer on credit

Bank Account
– records the money paid out
BANK

a business pays the advertising bill from the bank account

Notes
- in Sage the Bank accounts are listed in Nominal codes but are dealt with separately through the Bank accounts icon
- VAT is ignored here for the sake of simplicity

INPUT INTO A COMPUTER ACCOUNTING PACKAGE

manual input

Input into a computer accounting package is normally made direct on-screen from source documents or other data. If you are not familiar with financial documents, please read pages 71 to 75 before proceeding any further.

Typical transactions which form the 'bread and butter' of computer accounting input include:

- processing **sales invoices**, often in runs of several transactions known as 'batches' – the invoices are either produced before input or they can be input and printed out by the computer

- inputting **credit notes** from authorised documentation which says why the credit note has to be issued and a refund made – again the credit notes may be produced separately and used as a basis for input, or they may be printed out by the computer

- inputting **bank receipts** (money paid into the bank) – for example payments received from customers in settlement of accounts due

- inputting details of **new customer accounts** – this is the input of text onto what is effectively a database screen in the computer accounting package

There are, of course, many other types of transactions which you will input on the computer, but these are common examples. We will cover the input procedures in much greater detail in the individual chapters of this book.

importing data

Text files such as Customer and Supplier details can be imported into a computer accounting package from other programs such as Microsoft Office or other accounting programs.

authorisation and checking

Each organisation will have its own procedures to make sure that the data input is accurate and authorised. Source documents – invoices received, for example – may have a stamp placed on them with boxes for the initials of:

- the person checking the document

- the person authorising the input – often as part of a 'batch' of invoices

- the computer operator

- the person who checks the input against the source document

This ensures that accuracy is maintained. Each individual takes responsibility for a particular stage in the process and any errors can be traced to that individual.

OUTPUT FROM A COMPUTER ACCOUNTING PACKAGE

Output of data from a computer accounting package can take a number of different formats and can be used in a number of different ways.

printouts

The familiar form of data output from a computer is the paper printout. This is often referred to as 'hard copy'. There are a number of different forms of printout:

- day-to-day lists of items processed, eg a list of invoices produced on a particular day, a list of payments to suppliers

- financial documents such as invoices and credit notes

- reports for management, eg activity reports on accounts, aged debtors analysis (a list of who owes what – highlighting overdue accounts)

A printout of sales invoices produced is shown below.

Date:							Tapper Timber				Page: 1	
Time:							Day Books: Customer Invoices (Detailed)					

Date From:	04/07/2016								Customer From:		
Date To:	07/07/2016								Customer To:	ZZZZZZZZ	
Transaction From:	1								N/C From:		
Transaction To:	99,999,999								N/C To:	99999999	
Dept From:	0										
Dept To:	999										

Tran No.	Type	Date	A/C Ref	N/C	Inv Ref	Dept.	Details	Net Amount	Tax Amount	T/C	Gross Amount	V	B
25	SI	04/07/2016	VH001	4001	10023	0	Garden furniture	2,400.00	480.00	T1	2,880.00	N	-
26	SI	05/07/2016	OC001	4000	10024	0	Stock fencing	658.25	131.65	T1	789.90	N	-
27	SI	07/07/2016	CS001	4002	10025	0	Tack shed	5,740.00	1,148.00	T1	6,888.00	N	-
							Totals:	8,798.25	1,759.65		10,557.90		

emailed data

Most computer accounting packages have the facility for data to be exported to an email management program so that it can be emailed direct to the person who needs the information. Sage, for example, allows you to send invoices and statements direct to customers. Printouts and reports previewed on-screen can be emailed directly to external email addresses.

exporting data direct to other programs

Most computer accounting packages also allow you to export data to spreadsheet and word processing programs. Sage allows you to:

- export data to a Microsoft Excel spreadsheet, eg a list of the nominal accounts and their balances – this data will be placed direct into a spreadsheet grid from the Sage screen and can then be manipulated as required

- email reports in various formats from reports previewed on-screen

- export data files to your accountant

USING PASSWORDS

Before getting going on the computer you are likely to have to use **passwords** to enable you to gain access to:

- the computer itself, for example if you are using a workstation on a network – this is a **system password**

- particular computer programs, some of which may enable you to access sensitive or confidential information – eg the accounting software – this is a **software password**

system passwords – logging on

If you are working on a network you have to 'log on' as a user before you can use a computer workstation. You may have to give a user name and also a unique password. The user name will normally show on the screen as you input it, but the password will show as a series of dots or asterisks. The example below shows someone logging onto a computer in the production department.

logging onto the system

software passwords – accessing a program

Passwords are also needed to protect sensitive and confidential data held on the computer system. This is particularly important in the areas of staff records and also in the case of financial data processed by computer accounting programs.

One solution to the problem of unauthorised employees gaining access to sensitive financial data is the use of **passwords** to gain access to the computer program. Many larger businesses will employ a number of people who need to operate the computer accounting system; they will be issued with an appropriate password. Businesses can also set up **access rights** which restrict certain employees to certain activities and prevent them from accessing more sensitive areas such as the making of payments from the bank account.

When an employee comes to operate a computer accounting package, he or she will be asked to 'log on'. In the example from Sage shown below a person called R Tapper enters his logon name and a password.

DEALING WITH DATES

the different dates

One potential problem area for the operator of a computer accounting system is the use of dates when inputting. There are a number of dates that need to be considered:

■ the **system date** – this is the date that the computer thinks it is – usually the actual date

■ the **program date** – the date which you can instruct the accounting software to use as the actual date

■ the **financial year** start date – the month in which the financial year of the business starts

logging on and using dates

When you log on and start using the computer accounting software, you should check that the date shown at the bottom of the screen is the date you want to use for your input.

The date shown here will be allocated to any transactions that you input into the computer. Normally this is the **system date** (the date the computer thinks it is).

You should then ask yourself if you want your transactions to be allocated any other date. This might be the case if:

■ you are inputting a batch of transactions which went through last week – for example a number of payments received from customers – and you want the transactions to show on the records as going through last week

■ you are in a training situation and you have been given a specific date for input

If you are using Sage software in these cases you should change the **program date** through the SETTINGS menu. The program date lets you set any date to be 'today's date'.

This new date will appear against every transaction you make that day and will remain in force until you exit from the program, after which it reverts to the system (actual) date.

financial year

A business will use a financial year for accounting purposes. The financial year, like the calendar year, may run from January through to December. But the financial year can start anytime during the year; some businesses end their financial year on 31 March or 30 June, for example. When setting up the data in a computer accounting program you have to state when the financial year starts. In Sage this is done from the SETTINGS menu (see next page):

The financial year is important for the management of the business. Periodic and end-of-year routines provide the data from which financial statements and management reports can be produced.

SAVING AND BACK-UP

The computer accounting program you are using will tell you when to save your work. This is normally done after inputting a group of transactions and before passing on to the next task.

backing-up files

You will also need to **back-up** the data generated by the computer. There is no set rule about when you should do this, but it should be at least at the end of every day and preferably when you have completed a long run of inputting.

back-up media

Back-up files should be saved to some form of storage device.

Data can be backed up onto a variety of media:

- DVD or CD
- tape drive
- portable hard disk drive
- USB flash drive
- online storage/cloud

back-up in Sage

Back-up in Sage is carried out from the FILE menu, or on the prompt when you close down. The screen offers you a default file name which you can overwrite and asks to which drive you want the data saved. In the Sage screen shown at the top of the next page it is an external USB drive.

Clicking on Advanced Options allows you to decide which file types to back up. Data Files only is adequate for our purposes and takes up less storage space.

Back up ✕

- Back up company
- Advanced options
- Previous backups

Company details

You are about to create a backup of:

Company name: Tapper Timber

Found in: C:\PROGRAMDATA\SAGE\ACCOUNTS\2016\COMPANY.000\

Where do you want the company backed up to?

To select a location to save this backup to, click Browse. We have suggested a filename for this backup. If you are happy with this suggestion, click OK.

Backing up to removable media? Insert the device before clicking OK.

The Backup manager can back up your data automatically. For more information, press F1.

Filename*: backup 31 07 16

Location*: F:\

Browse...

OK   Cancel   Help

Back up ✕

- Back up company
- Advanced options
- Previous backups

File types to include in backup

Type	Included?
Data Files	✓
Report Files	☐
Layout Templates	☐
Attachments	☐
Image Files	☐
Company Archives	☐
TMail Database	☐

☐ Select all file types to include in backup

Description of backup for Tapper Timber

Backup of :
  - Data Files.
Backup created by MANAGER 05/01/2016

OK   Cancel   Help

If you are using Sage you are recommended to run the ERROR CHECKING routine from MAINTENANCE (from the FILE menu) before backing up. This will check the data files and ensure that you do not back-up any corrupted data. The two screens involved look like these:

File Maintenance Problems Report ✕

Recovery tools   Print

Summary
Errors
Warnings
Comments
Technical Information

Errors

❌ No errors found.

Warnings

⚠ No warnings generated.

Comments

ℹ No comments made.

❓ How to fix errors & warnings in your Sage data   Close

File maintenance ✕

Error checking
Your data was last checked on: 01/07/2016. It is recommended you run this option on a regular basis.

Last Results

Data compression
If you have previously deleted large amounts of data, run this option to reclaim disk space used by deleted records.

Compress Data

Recovery Tools
Choose this option if y[...] warnings in your data. [...] caution.

Check Complete ✕

No problems to report on data files.

OK

[...]on to erase data files and [...]h. Use with extreme caution.

Rebuild

Reindex data files
This option allows you to create new indexes for your ledger files.

Reindex

Close

back-up policy

It is important that an organisation works out a systematic policy for back-up of its data. This should involve:

- more than one back-up held at any one time

- back-up media held off the premises

- periodic back-up (eg back-ups at the end of each month) stored securely

One solution is for the business to keep a set of back-up media for each working day, labelled with the name of the day.

At the end of each working day the data is backed up on the appropriate back-up media, which are kept securely on site, preferably under lock and key.

As a further security measure, a second set of back-ups could be kept as an off-site security back-up. These would be backed up at the end of each day and taken off-site by an employee, or stored online.

With this system in place the business has double security for its valuable data.

It should also be mentioned that the back-up media should be replaced periodically (every three months, for example) as they wear out in time and the data can become corrupted.

restoring data from a back-up

In the unfortunate event that the accounting data on your computer has been lost or corrupted, you can **restore** the data from an earlier date from the appropriate back-up media. This is carried out in Sage from RESTORE in the FILE menu. Note that all the data is restored in this process; it is not possible to restore selected files. You should then run ERROR CHECKING routine from FILE MAIN-TENANCE to make sure the restored data is not corrupted.

Restore

Restore company
Previous backups

Which backup do you want to restore?

If this is on a removable storage device, insert this now.

File*: F:\backup 31 07 16.001   Browse...

Description of data to be restored for: Tapper Timber

Tapper Timber
Backup of :
 - Data Files.

Backup details

Company name: Tapper Timber

Data version: V22

Your backup will be restored to

Company name: Tapper Timber

Location: C:\PROGRAMDATA\SAGE\ACCOUNTS\2016\COMPANY.000\

OK   Cancel   Help

SOFTWARE PROBLEMS

Software problems can occur. If it is a case of not knowing how to carry out a particular operation, refer the matter to someone who does. Help is always at hand through HELP menus, on line support or telephone technical support to which the business is likely to have subscribed. If a program crashes, it may be necessary to restart the computer. If the program refuses to work after repeated attempts, it may have become corrupted, in which case it may need to be re-installed.

corrupted, deleted or overwritten data files

Problems can also be caused if a data file:

- becomes **corrupt**, ie it becomes unusable and will not open or print, or both
- gets **deleted** by accident or by a malicious computer virus
- is accidentally **overwritten** by an older version of a file, and in the process wipes out the work you may have done on the file

In these cases you have to rely on being able to restore your back-up files.

virus protection

Computers are vulnerable to viruses. A **virus** is a destructive program which can be introduced into the computer either from a disk, USB memory stick, an internet download, email attachment or from another computer.

Some viruses are relatively harmless and may merely display messages on the screen, others can be very damaging and destroy operating systems and data, putting the computer system completely out of action. Most computers are now sold already installed with virus protection software which will:

- establish a firewall to repel viruses
- check for existing viruses
- destroy known viruses
- check for damage to files on the hard disk
- repair damage to files on the hard disk where possible

This software should be run and updated regularly so that it can deal with the latest viruses.

precautions against viruses

There are a number of precautions which you can take against viruses:

- be wary of opening unidentified email attachments

■ use protective software to inspect any disk or memory stick received from an outside source before opening up any file saved onto it

■ make sure that your protective software is up to date – very often they will update automatically over the internet

If your protective software announces that you have a virus, you should report it at once in your workplace and stop using your computer.

Chapter Summary

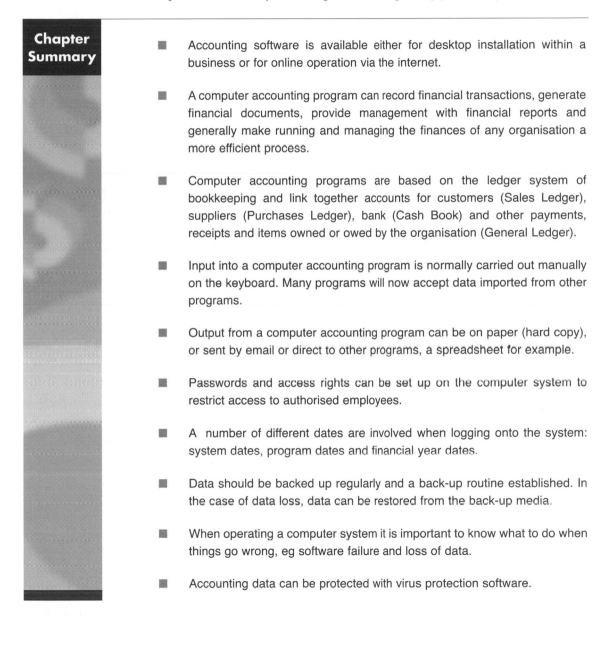

■ Accounting software is available either for desktop installation within a business or for online operation via the internet.

■ A computer accounting program can record financial transactions, generate financial documents, provide management with financial reports and generally make running and managing the finances of any organisation a more efficient process.

■ Computer accounting programs are based on the ledger system of bookkeeping and link together accounts for customers (Sales Ledger), suppliers (Purchases Ledger), bank (Cash Book) and other payments, receipts and items owned or owed by the organisation (General Ledger).

■ Input into a computer accounting program is normally carried out manually on the keyboard. Many programs will now accept data imported from other programs.

■ Output from a computer accounting program can be on paper (hard copy), or sent by email or direct to other programs, a spreadsheet for example.

■ Passwords and access rights can be set up on the computer system to restrict access to authorised employees.

■ A number of different dates are involved when logging onto the system: system dates, program dates and financial year dates.

■ Data should be backed up regularly and a back-up routine established. In the case of data loss, data can be restored from the back-up media.

■ When operating a computer system it is important to know what to do when things go wrong, eg software failure and loss of data.

■ Accounting data can be protected with virus protection software.

Key Terms		
	desktop software	software that is installed and maintained within a business computer system
	cloud-based software	software that is accessed and maintained online
	ledgers	the books of the accounting system which contain individual accounts – the Sales Ledger, for example, contains the individual accounts of customers who buy on credit (ie they pay later)
	integrated system	a computerised accounting system which links together all the ledgers and accounts so that a transaction on one account will always be mirrored in another account
	double-entry bookkeeping	the method of manual bookkeeping from which the integrated system has been developed – it involves the making of two entries in the accounts for every financial transaction
	hard copy	a paper document containing data – often a printout from a computer
	data export	the transfer of data from one computer program to another
	system password	a code word used to allow an employee to 'log on' to access the computer accounting system
	software password	a code word used to allow an employee to 'log on' to access a particular computer accounting program, such as Sage
	access rights	the right of an employee to access specified areas of the computer accounting program
	system date	the date allocated by the operating system of the computer – normally the actual date
	program date	the date which you can tell the computer accounting software to use as 'today's' date
	financial year	the twelve-month period used by the business to record its financial transactions
	back-up	to copy the computer data onto a separate storage medium in order to ensure that the data is not lost

restore	to copy the back-up data back onto the computer when the original data has been lost or corrupted
corrupt data	data which has become unusable
virus	a computer program introduced into the computer system which then disrupts or destroys the operation of the system

Activities

1.1 Explain how passwords and access rights to accounting software help protect computer data.

1.2 Explain the difference between a system date and a program date used on a computer accounting program.

1.3 Write down a suggested back-up policy for an office which runs a computer accounting system.

1.4 You are running a check on your computer accounting data at the end of the day before carrying out the back-up routine. The message appears on-screen that a number of your data files have become corrupted. You normally back-up your data daily at the end of the day. Explain what you would do to rescue your data and bring the computer accounting records up to date.

1.5 You hear from a friend working for another business that their computer systems have had a catastrophic crash following infection by a virus which came in over the internet. Describe the measures you could take to safeguard against a similar catastrophe to your own systems.

2 Setting up the business

this chapter covers...

- Setting up a computer accounting program for a business or other organisation will take some time, but as long as the correct data is entered in the correct format there should be no problem.

- We will assume here that the organisation setting up the computer accounting program is a business.

- The chapter introduces a Case Study business – Tapper Timber – which will be used throughout this book to show how computer accounting works.

- There is plenty of help around when you are setting up accounts on the computer. In Sage, for example, there is the user guide, the 'Help' function, and on-screen step-by-step instruction procedures known as 'Wizards'.

- The data that will have to be input includes:

    - the business details such as name and address, financial year and VAT status

    - the customer details and any sales transactions outstanding

    - the supplier details and any purchases transactions outstanding

    - details of accounts for income and expenses, assets (items owned), liabilities (loans) and capital (money put in by the owner) – these are all contained in the general ledger

- This chapter concentrates on setting up the business details. The other data – customer and supplier details and balances and the general ledger – will be covered in the next two chapters.

> **important note**
> AAT assessments will require the setting up of business details and financial year, together with the ability to set the software date (p10). Assistance can be given by the training provider because this aspect of set-up does not form part of the standards, but it is useful for candidates to know how to enter set-up details.

WHERE ARE YOU STARTING FROM?

If you are reading this book you are likely to be in one of two situations:

1   You are in a real business and looking for guidance in setting up a computer accounting system.

2   You are a student in a training situation and will have the program already set up for you on a training centre network. You will be given exercises to practise using a computer accounting program.

In the first case – the real business – you may be starting from scratch and will have to go through the whole installation and set-up procedure. This is not at all difficult. The software itself will take you through the various steps.

In the second case – the training centre situation – the computer may already have accounting records on it, possibly another student's work. You will need to refer to your training provider on how to set up your data.

The Case Study which follows on the next page – Tapper Timber – assumes that you are in business setting up computer accounts for the first time using Sage software. It is important for your studies that you know how this is done, even if you may not carry out in the training centre all the procedures explained in the Case Study.

WHY SAGE AND WHICH SAGE?

Osborne Books (the publisher of this book) has chosen Sage software for this book for two very good reasons:

1   Sage software is widely used in business and is recognised as a user-friendly and reliable product.

2   Osborne Books has used Sage itself for many years and is familiar with the way it works.

The Sage software used as a basis for this book is Sage 50 Accounts Professional (Version 22). The screens displayed in this book are taken from this version by kind permission of Sage (UK) Limited.

screen illustrations

It should be appreciated that some training centres and businesses may be using older and slightly different versions of Sage and so some of the screens may look slightly different. This does not matter however: using Sage is like driving different models of car – the controls may be located in slightly different places and the dashboard may not look exactly the same, but the controls are still there and they still do the same thing. So if the screens shown here look unfamiliar, examine them carefully and you will see that they will contain the same (or very similar) Sage icons and functions as the version you are using.

Case Study

TAPPER TIMBER:
SETTING UP THE BUSINESS

the business

Ross Tapper owns and runs a business called Tapper Timber. He operates as a sole trader in the town of Stourcastle. The business manufactures and sells fencing, garden furniture and sheds to local farms, businesses and households. The business operates from Unit 3, Greenslade Way, Stourcastle, ST4 6TG.

Tapper Timber offers credit terms of 30 days to all its customers and it is VAT-registered. All its products are standard-rated for VAT.

The financial year of the business starts on 1 July.

the accounting system

Tapper Timber's accounts have been run manually since Ross started the business two years ago. Ross has decided to computerise his manual accounts from 1 July 2016 so that he can record:

- sales invoices issued to his credit customers
- purchase invoices received from his credit suppliers
- bank receipts and payments
- income and expenses, business assets and loans

In short he will have an integrated computer accounting system enabling him to:

- Record all his financial transactions
- Print out reports
- Manage his business finances
- Save time (and money)

getting started

Ross installs the program and uses the ActiveSetup Wizard to take him through the set up procedure.

A Wizard is a series of dialogue boxes on the screen which takes you step-by-step through a particular procedure. The ActiveSetup Wizard is one of a number of wizards in Sage. Wizards generally appear automatically on-screen when you need to carry out a complex process.

Ross is taken through a series of screens by which he can personalise the program to his business. In the first he chooses to set up a new company as shown below.

```
ActiveSetup                                                            ✕

Sage Accounts - Company Set-up

  1  Welcome      Welcome to Sage 50 Accounts                          ❓
                  Please select one of the following:

                    ◉ Set-up a new company                         ❓
                    ○ Use an existing company stored on your network ❓
                    ○ Restore data from a backup file               ❓
                    ○ Connect to data from Sage Drive               ❓

                  Your company will be created in the following location.
                  C:\PROGRAMDATA\SAGE\ACCOUNTS\2016\COMPANY.000\   [ Change ]
```

Next he must enter his business details.

```
ActiveSetup                                                            ✕

Sage Accounts - Company Set-up

  1  Welcome          Enter Company Details ❓                          ❓

  2  Network Sharing  Company Name :   Tapper Timber
                      Street 1 :       Unit 3
  3  Company Details  Street 2 :       Greenslade Way
                      Town :           Stourcastle
  4  Business Type    County :
                      Post Code :      ST4 6TG
  5  Financial Year
                      Country :        United Kingdom    GB          ⌄
  6  VAT              Telephone Number : 01877 453611
                      Fax Number :       01877 453286
  7  Currency         Email Address :    info@tappertimber.co.uk
                      Website Address :  www.tappertimber.co.uk
  8  Manager Password

  9  Confirm Details

  [ Cancel ]                                         [ Back ]  [ Next ]
```

Ross is a sole trader so he chooses this option from the Business Type choices.

Next he sets up his financial year start date: July 2016

The next two screens require Ross to enter the business VAT details and the currency he trades in. Finally, he must enter the serial number and activation key provided by Sage to activate the program.

At this stage Ross could enter a password to override the default settings in Sage (see image on the next page).

ActiveSetup   ×

Sage Accounts - Company Set-up

1 Welcome

2 Network Sharing

3 Company Details

4 Business Type

5 Financial Year

6 VAT

7 Currency

8 **Manager Password**

9 Confirm Details

Manager Password

The default login for Sage 50 Accounts is "Manager". This gives you full access to all features. We strongly recommend that you set a password for the default login now. You can create further logins later.

Enter Password   [   ]

Confirm Password   [   ]

The password can be up to ten characters long and can include spaces and numbers.

Cancel   Back   Next

He can now confirm the details he has entered and log on to the program.

ActiveSetup   ×

Sage Accounts - Company Set-up

1 Welcome

2 Network Sharing

3 Company Details

4 Business Type

5 Financial Year

6 VAT

7 Currency

8 Manager Password

9 **Confirm Details**

Create

You must confirm that the key details below are correct. Click Back to make changes or click Create to create your company.

What you have entered

Share location:	\\DESKTOP-NGD803S\SAGE2016
Share this folder?	Yes
Company Name:	Tapper Timber
Business Type:	Sole Trader
Financial Year:	01 July 2016 - 30 June 2017
VAT Scheme:	Standard VAT
Currency:	Pound Sterling

Cancel   Back   Create

Ross can close the 'Customise Your Company' option. He will be customising it as we move on through the Case Study.

Now Ross should check his VAT codes. He can do this by selecting CONFIGURATION from the SETTINGS menu. The VAT defaults are shown on the Tax codes tab. They are the correct codes for Ross to use: T1 for standard rate, T0 for zero-rated transactions (eg sales of books), T2 for exempt transactions and T9 for non-VAT items. The screen appears as follows.

Configuration Editor ✕

| Fixed Assets | Custom Fields | Dispute Reasons | Credit Control | Project Costing |
| General | Chart of Accounts | Terms | Tax Codes | Account Status | Products |

Tax Codes

Sage 50 Accounts helps you to keep track of VAT with a comprehensive set of tax codes. These tax codes are set-up by default when you install the program, and you will not normally need to change any of the settings.

If you do need to modify any of the tax codes, you can do this below.

For more information on VAT and tax codes, visit the HM Revenue and Customs web site - just select "HM Revenue and Customs" from the WebLinks menu.

Code	Rate	In Use	EC Sales	EC Purchases	Description
T0	0.00	Y	N	N	Zero rated transactions
T1	20.00	Y	N	N	Standard rated transactions
T2	0.00	Y	N	N	Exempt transactions
T3	0.00	Y	N	N	
T4	0.00	Y	Y	N	Sales of goods to VAT registered customers ...
T5	5.00	Y	N	N	Lower Rate
T6	0.00	Y	N	N	

[Edit]

Company Preferences ✕

| Budgeting | VAT | Sage Pay | Sage Payments |
| Details | Labels | Parameters | Reporting | Accountant |

Name	Tapper Timber
Street1	Unit 3
Street2	Greenslade Way
Town	Stourcastle
County	
Post Code	ST4 6TG
Country	United Kingdom GB
Telephone	01877 453611
Fax	01877 453786
Email	info@tappertimber.co.uk
Website	www.tappertimber.co.uk
Credit Ref	
DUNS Number	

[Delivery Addresses...]

The business details entered can be checked or amended at any time via COMPANY PREFERENCES in the SETTINGS menu. The screen is illustrated on the left.

There are a number of tabs, including Details. The details entered here will automatically be printed on business documents such as customer statements. Ross could enter a different delivery address on this tab if needed. He does not need to enter anything else in COMPANY PREFERENCES at this stage.

When Ross opens his accounting software program again, he will be faced with a different screen (see next page) asking him to choose the business he wants to open. He can simply select Tapper Timber and click OK.

After entering his logon name and password (if one is required) the program will open ready for data input.

ON-SCREEN HELP

Ross now has his business details set up on the computer but he still has to install his account balances and get to know how the system works. Sage provides on-screen help for the user.

On-screen help can be accessed through either the HELP menu or by pressing the F1 function key. Look at the diagram below.

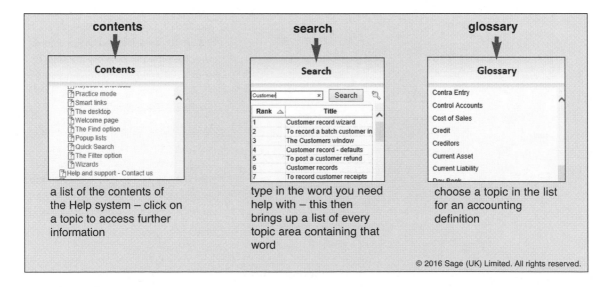

contents

a list of the contents of the Help system – click on a topic to access further information

search

type in the word you need help with – this then brings up a list of every topic area containing that word

glossary

choose a topic in the list for an accounting definition

TRANSFERRING DATA INTO SAGE

When a business first sets up a computer accounting system a substantial amount of data will need to be transferred onto the computer, even if the business is in its first week of trading. A summary of this data is shown in the diagram below.

The images shown in the diagram are the icons on the Sage desktop which represent the different operating areas of the program. As you can see they relate to the ledger structure of a manual bookkeeping system.

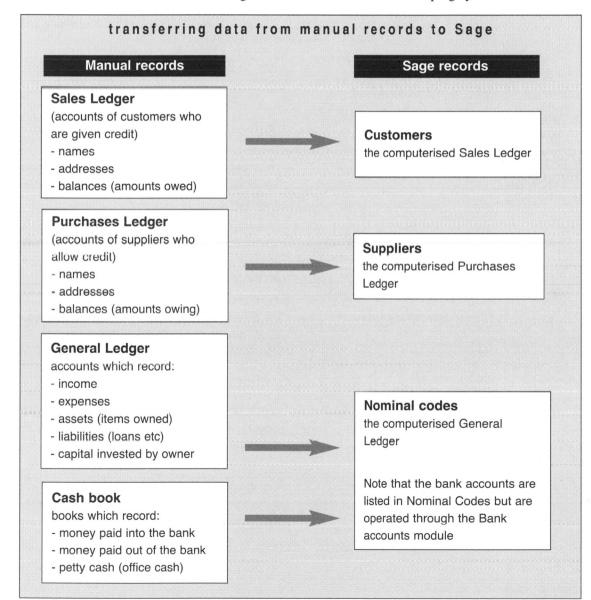

transferring data from manual records to Sage

Manual records

Sage records

Sales Ledger
(accounts of customers who are given credit)
- names
- addresses
- balances (amounts owed)

Customers
the computerised Sales Ledger

Purchases Ledger
(accounts of suppliers who allow credit)
- names
- addresses
- balances (amounts owing)

Suppliers
the computerised Purchases Ledger

General Ledger
accounts which record:
- income
- expenses
- assets (items owned)
- liabilities (loans etc)
- capital invested by owner

Cash book
books which record:
- money paid into the bank
- money paid out of the bank
- petty cash (office cash)

Nominal codes
the computerised General Ledger

Note that the bank accounts are listed in Nominal Codes but are operated through the Bank accounts module

Chapter Summary

■ A business setting up a computer accounting program for the first time will have to enter the details of the business on-screen, for example:

- the business name and address
- the start date of the financial year of the business
- the business VAT registration number and VAT Status (where applicable)
- any passwords that are needed
- the program serial number and Activation Key code

■ The business type will also be required so that the correct 'chart of accounts' is loaded – this is the list of Nominal codes which will automatically be set up on the system.

■ The business can make use of the on-screen Wizard and other 'Help' functions in the set-up process.

Key Terms

Wizard — on-screen dialogue boxes in a Sage program which take you step-by-step through complex procedures

sales ledger — the accounts of customers to whom a business sells on credit – in Sage this part of the accounting system is known as 'Customers'

purchases ledger — the accounts of suppliers from whom a business buys on credit – in Sage this part of the accounting system is known as 'Suppliers'

general ledger — the remaining accounts in the accounting system which are not Customers or Suppliers, eg income, expenses, assets, liabilities – in Sage this is known as 'Nominal'

chart of accounts — the structure of the nominal accounts, which groups accounts into categories such as Sales, Purchases, Overheads etc

Activities

2.1 Describe the sources of assistance that are available to Alan Bramley who is setting up a Sage system for the first time.

2.2 Helen Egremont is setting up a Sage system for the first time. What details will have to be input before any account balances can be transferred?

2.3 James Greave has been trading for six months using a manual double-entry bookkeeping system. Into what part of a Sage system will the following ledgers be transferred?

(a) Sales Ledger

(b) Purchases Ledger

(c) General Ledger

TAPPER TIMBER INPUTTING TASK

important notes

1   This activity involves you in setting up a new company in Sage and inputting data into the computer.

2   It may be that the business has already been set up for you on the computer or that you have to carry out a 'Restore' operation to set up the company. If this is the case, you should ignore these two tasks.

Task 1

Set the program date as 1 July 2016. Set up the business details of Tapper Timber. The details are:

Address/contact details	Unit 3, Greenslade Way, Stourcastle. ST4 6TG
	Tel 01877 453611 Fax 01877 453286
	Email info@tappertimber.co.uk
	www.tappertimber.co.uk
Business type	Sole trader
Financial year start	July 2016
VAT registration number	404 7106 52

Task 2

Check the business details in the first tab of COMPANY PREFERENCES in SETTINGS.

Now check that the Details tab in COMPANY PREFERENCES matches the screen on page 27. Make any amendments if you need to.

Reminder! Have you made a back-up?

3 Setting up records for customers and suppliers

this chapter covers...

- The term 'Customers' means people to whom a business sells on credit. In other words, the goods or services are supplied straightaway and the customer is allowed to pay at a specified later date – often a month or more later. Another term for a credit customer is a 'receivable' (debtor).

- A business keeps running accounts for the amounts owed by individual customers – much as a bank keeps accounts for its customers. The accounts are maintained by the business in the 'Sales Ledger'.

- The term 'Suppliers' means people from whom a business buys on credit. In other words, the goods or services are supplied straightaway and the business is allowed to pay at a specified later date. Another term for a credit supplier is a 'payable' (creditor).

- A business keeps running accounts for the amounts owed to individual suppliers. The accounts are maintained by the business in the 'Purchases Ledger'.

- This chapter continues the Tapper Timber Case Study and shows how the business sets up its Customer and Supplier records on the computer.

- When the accounts have been set up on the computer the business will need to input the amounts currently owed by Customers and owing to Suppliers.

CASH AND CREDIT SALES

cash and credit – the difference

When businesses such as manufacturers, shops and travel agents sell their products, they will either get their money straightaway, or they will receive the money after an agreed time period. The first type of sale is a **cash sale**, the second is a **credit sale**. These can be defined further as:

cash sale A sale of a product where the money is received straightaway – this can include payment in cash, by cheque or by credit card and debit card. The word 'cash' means 'immediate' – it does not mean only notes and coins.

credit sale A sale of a product or service where the sale is agreed and the goods or services are supplied but the buyer pays at a later date agreed at the time of the sale.

buying and selling for cash and on credit

Businesses are likely to get involved in cash and credit sales not only when they are selling their products but also when they are buying. Some goods and services will be bought for cash and some on credit. Buying and selling are just two sides of the same operation.

You will see from this that it is the nature of the business that will decide what type of sales and purchases it makes. A supermarket, for example, will sell almost entirely for cash – the cash and credit/debit card payments come in at the checkouts – and it will buy from its suppliers on credit and pay them later. It should therefore always have money in hand – which is a good situation to be in for a business.

SETTING UP CUSTOMER ACCOUNTS

accounting records for customers

Customers who buy from a business on credit are known as **receivables** (**debtors**) because they owe money to the business and the business will in due course 'receive' it.

The amounts owed by customers are recorded in individual customer accounts in the **Sales Ledger**. In double-entry terms these customer account balances are **debit balances**.

The total of all the customer (receivable/debtor) accounts in the Sales Ledger is recorded in an account known as **Debtors Control Account**. This is the total amount owing by the customers of a business.

accounting records for suppliers

When a business purchases goods and services from its suppliers on credit the suppliers are known as **payables** (**creditors**) because the business owes them money and has to 'pay' them.

The amounts owed to suppliers (payables/creditors) are recorded in individual supplier accounts in the **Purchases Ledger**. In double-entry terms these supplier account balances are **credit balances**.

The total of all the supplier accounts in the Purchases Ledger is known as **Creditors Control Account**. This is the total amount owing to the suppliers of a business.

All this is summarised in the table set out below.

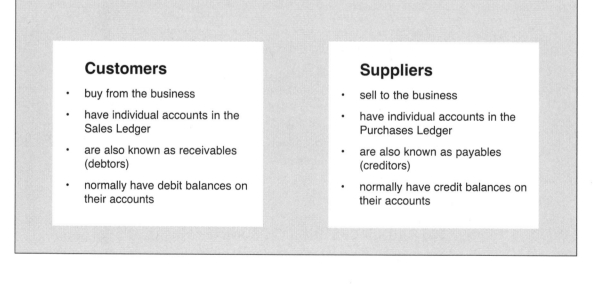

Customers

- buy from the business
- have individual accounts in the Sales Ledger
- are also known as receivables (debtors)
- normally have debit balances on their accounts

Suppliers

- sell to the business
- have individual accounts in the Purchases Ledger
- are also known as payables (creditors)
- normally have credit balances on their accounts

credit limits

When a business is opening a new account it will need to establish a credit limit. A **credit limit** is the maximum amount of credit a seller is willing to grant to a customer. For example if a credit limit of £5,000 is set up by the seller, the customer can owe up to £5,000 at any one time – for example two invoices of £2,500. A well-managed business will keep an eye on situations where a credit limit might be exceeded.

credit terms

The seller will need to establish its **terms** of trading with its customers and the customer will have to agree. The terms are normally set out on the invoice (the invoice is the document issued when the goods or services are sold and supplied). They include:

- **trade discount** given to the customer based on the selling price, for example a customer with a 30% trade discount will pay £70 for goods costing £100, ie £100 minus £30 (30% discount)

- the **payment terms** – the length of credit allowed to the customer, ie the number of days the customer is allowed to wait before paying up – this is commonly 30 days after the invoice date

- **settlement discount** (also known as **cash discount**) sometimes given to a customer who settles up early within a specified number of days, for example a 2.5% reduction for settlement within 7 days

day-to-day customer/supplier information

A business will need information on file relating to its day-to-day dealings with customers and suppliers. For example:

- the name and address of the customer

- telephone and fax numbers, email, and website address (if there is one)

- contact names

- credit limit, trade discount, payment terms and any settlement discount agreed

setting up the accounts

As you will see from the last three pages, there is a great deal of information that has to be input when setting up accounts for customers and suppliers on a computer accounting program such as Sage.

In the Case Study which follows on page 40 we will follow the steps taken by Tapper Timber in setting up its Customers and Suppliers records.

SETTING UP THE COMPUTER FILES

There are two methods in Sage for setting up new records for customers or suppliers. If, for example, you wanted to set up a new Customer account you could:

1 Go to the CUSTOMERS screen and click on WIZARD. You will be given a Wizard to take you through the procedure.

2 Go to the CUSTOMERS screen and click on NEW. You will be given a blank screen to complete, but with no Wizard guidance.

The Wizard screen is shown below and the second method is illustrated in the Case Study, as the process is very simple.

Whether you are using the Wizard or just setting up a new record through NEW, you will need to have to hand all the customer details you have on file. These are the type of details covered earlier in this chapter.

customer and supplier reference codes

You will see from the Wizard screen shown above that you need to decide on a unique reference code for each customer and supplier account. This code can be letters, numbers, or a mixture of both. If letters are used they are often an abbreviation of the account name. This process, using both letters and numbers, will be illustrated in the Case Study.

customer and supplier record defaults

If you are setting up a number of customer and supplier accounts it is possible that the terms agreed – discounts and payment periods – will be the same for each customer or supplier account. To save you entering these in each and every account (which can take a lot of time!) you can establish a default set of terms which will apply to all accounts. These can be set up from the 'Terms' tab of the CONFIGURATION EDITOR in SETTINGS.

It is also important to establish the standard VAT rate to be used in transactions (currently 20%) and also the default account number used for sales to customers (usually account number 4000). This is carried out from the 'Record' tab in CUSTOMER DEFAULTS in SETTINGS. In the illustration below note the default VAT code (T1, 20%) and the 'Def. N/C' default Sales Account number 4000 (N/C stands for 'Nominal Code').

TAPPER TIMBER:
SETTING UP CUSTOMERS AND SUPPLIERS

Ross Tapper has decided to input his customer and supplier records into the system first, and then afterwards he will input the General ledger balances.

There are three customer accounts and three supplier accounts.

Customers

Account reference	Account name	Amount outstanding £
OC001	Oliver Cole & Sons	2,904.20
VH001	Victoria Hotel	9,900.78
CS001	Cornwood Stud	5,726.88
		18,531.86

The total outstanding from customers as at 1 July 2016 is £18,531.86.

Suppliers

Account reference	Account name	Amount owing £
CP001	Chapman Panels	6,242.52
ET001	Estate Timber Ltd	4,506.00
JF001	Johnsons Fixings	5,006.82
		15,755.34

The total owing to suppliers as at 1 July 2016 is £15,755.34.

entering the customer defaults

Ross sets his program date to 1 July 2016. He decides that he will save time by setting up his standard terms in the CONFIGURATION EDITOR in SETTINGS:

Payment due days   30 days

Terms of payment   Payment 30 days of invoice

See image at the top of the next page.

He also checks his default VAT code (T1) and rate (20%) and Sales Account number (4000) in CUSTOMER DEFAULTS (reached through SETTINGS):

VAT rate   Standard rate of 20% (this is Tax Code T1)

Default nominal code   4000

Configuration Editor   ×

| Fixed Assets | Custom Fields | Dispute Reasons | | Credit Control | Project Costing |
| General | Chart of Accounts | Terms | Tax Codes | Account Status | Products |

Trading Terms

Sage 50 Accounts helps you to establish and record trading terms with your customers and suppliers. You can set default values for these trading terms below. These defaults will be used for any new customer and supplier accounts you create.

You can also set finance rates to be used on customers that you allow credit charges on.

Customer Trading Terms

Credit Limit	0.00	Payment Due	30	Days
Sett. Discount	0.00	Sett. Discount Due	0	Days
Terms	Payment 30 days of invoice			

Customer Finance Rates

There is currently no finance rate applying.

Date From	Base Rate (%)	Additional (%)

Supplier Trading Terms

Credit Limit	0.00	Payment Due	0	Days
Sett. Discount	0.00	Sett. Discount Due	0	Days
Terms				

Add   Edit   Delete

Save   Save As   Apply   Press 'Apply' to use this configuration on your accounts data.
Press 'Save' or 'Save As' to create a configuration file to use on other accounts data sets.   Close

Ross decides not to set a default credit limit as this will vary from customer to customer and will be input with the individual customer details.

Note also that Ross does not allow **discounts** on his sales nor receive discounts on his purchases.

entering customer details and opening balances

Ross now enters the details and the opening balances for each customer. He does this by clicking on NEW in CUSTOMERS. The first customer to input is Oliver Cole & Sons. The information to be input (including an outstanding invoice issued in June) is as follows:

Account name	Oliver Cole & Sons
Account reference	OC001
Address	Wood Farm, Collingwood ST8 6TF
Contact name	Jem Cole
Telephone	01908 824295
Email	jem@olivercole.co.uk
Credit limit	£5,000
Outstanding invoice	Invoice reference 10013 for £2,904.20 issued on 10 June 2016

Ross inputs the data on the 'Details' screen.

Account Details

A/C*	OC001
Company name	Oliver Cole & Sons
Balance	0.00
Inactive	☐

Registered Address

Street1	Wood Farm
Street2	
Town	Collingwood
County	
Post Code	ST8 6TF
Country	United Kingdom GB
VAT Number	

Addresses & Contacts...

Contact Information

Contact name	Jem Cole
Trade contact	
Telephone	01908 824295
Telephone 2	
Fax	
Website	

Email Settings & Addresses

Email 1	jem@olivercole.co.uk
Email2	
Email3	
I send letters, statements, etc. to this customer via email	☐
I send invoices to this customer via Transaction Email	☐

He now has to input the details of the invoice which he issued to Oliver Cole & Sons on 10 June which has not yet been paid. He does this by clicking the O/B button (in the Balance box below Company Name) which brings up the screen shown on the next page. When prompted to Save the new record, Ross clicks 'Yes'.

Account Details

A/C*	OC001
Company name	Oliver Cole & Sons
Balance	0.00
Inactive	☐

Registered Address

Street1	Wood Farm
Street2	
Town	Collingwood
County	
Post Code	ST8 6TF
Country	United Kingdom GB
VAT Number	

Addresses & Co...

Contact Information

Contact name	Jem Cole
Trade contact	
Telephone	01908 824295
Telephone 2	
Fax	
Website	

Opening Balance Setup   ✕

Ref	Date*	Type	Gross*
10013	10/06/2016	Invoice	2904.20

Save   Cancel

Ross inputs the following data into the above screen:

Ref: the invoice reference number

Date: the date the invoice was issued *

Type: the transaction was an invoice

Gross: the total amount of the invoice

*the program warns that this date is outside the current financial year – this is OK

Ross now goes to the CREDIT CONTROL screen of Oliver Cole's new record to input the customer credit limit, the payment period and terms. The terms may already be entered if the default customer terms have been entered. He ticks the box marked 'Terms agreed' and then hits Save.

Customer Record - Oliver Cole & Sons

Clear form | New invoice | New order | New project | Delete

- Details
- Defaults
- **Credit Control**
- Bank
- Communications
- Memo

- Activity
- Sales
- Orders
- Projects
- Graphs

Terms

Credit Limit	5000.00
Settlement Due	0 Days
Sett.Discount	0.00
Payment Due	30 Days
Average Time to Pay	28 Days
Trading Terms Text	Payment 30 days of invoi
Credit Ref.	...
Bureau	▾
Priority Customer	☐
Credit Position	Good ▾
Account status	0 Open ▾
DUNS Number	

Restrictions

☐ Can charge credit   ☐ Restrict mailing
☑ Terms agreed   ☐ Account On Hold

Ross now repeats this process for the other two customers.

entering supplier details and opening balances

Ross now carries out the same process for supplier details and opening balances. He first ensures that the supplier defaults include T1 as the default tax code and 5000 as the default nominal account code.

He sets up his supplier accounts by clicking on NEW in SUPPLIERS. The first supplier to input is Chapman Panels. The information to be input (including an outstanding invoice from June) is as follows:

Account name	Chapman Panels
Account reference	CP001
Address	17 Main Street, Martleford ST5 2BG
Contact name	Ella Chapman
Telephone	01722 295611
Email	sales@chapmanpanels.co.uk
Credit limit	£15,000
Outstanding invoice	Invoice reference 7611 for £6,242.52 dated 20 June 2016
Terms	Payment due 30 days

Ross inputs the supplier details and opening balances, starting with Chapman Panels. The completed details screen is shown below.

Supplier Record - Chapman Panels — □ ×

Clear form | New order | Delete

Details
Defaults
Credit Control
Bank
Communications
Memo

Activity
Purchases
Orders
Graphs

Account Details

A/C*: CP001
Company name: Chapman Panels
Balance: 6242.52
Inactive ☐

Registered address

Street1 17 Main Street
Street2
Town Martleford
County
Post Code ST5 2BG
Country United Kingdom GB
VAT Number

Addresses & Contacts...

Contact information

Contact name: Ella Chapman
Trade contact:
Telephone: 01722 295611
Telephone 2:
Fax:
Website:

Email Settings & Addresses

Email1 sales@chapmanpanels.co.uk
Email2
Email3

I send letters, remittances, etc to this supplier via email ☐
I send orders to this supplier via Transaction Email ☐

Ross now goes to the CREDIT CONTROL screen to input the credit limit imposed by the supplier, and the payment terms. He ticks the box marked 'Terms agreed' and then Saves again.

Supplier Record - Chapman Panels

Clear form   New order   Delete

Details
Defaults
Credit Control
Bank
Communications
Memo

Activity
Purchases
Orders
Graphs

Terms

Credit Limit	15000.00
Settlement Due	0 Days
Sett.Discount	0.00
Payment Due	30 Days
Trading Terms Text	
Credit Reference	
Bureau	
Priority Supplier	☐
Credit Position	Good
Account status	0 Open
DUNS Number	

Restrictions

☐ Can charge credit   ☐ Restrict mailing
☑ Terms agreed   ☐ Account On Hold

Ross now repeats this process for the other two suppliers.

the final checks

Ross checks that the customer and supplier details he has input are correct.

He prints out a Day Books: Customer Invoices (Detailed) report to check that customer opening balance details are accurate. To do this he goes back to the CUSTOMERS screen and ensures that none of the customers are selected (if any are, he clicks 'Clear' on the toolbar). He clicks REPORTS on the toolbar, chooses Day books and scrolls down to Day Books: Customer Invoices (Detailed). He double clicks it (or clicks the Preview icon) and leaves all the criteria values as default, then clicks OK.

Date: Time:		**Tapper Timber** **Day Books: Customer Invoices (Detailed)**									Page: 1	

Date From:	01/01/1980									Customer From:		
Date To:	31/12/2019									Customer To:	ZZZZZZZZ	
Transaction From:	1									N/C From:		
Transaction To:	99,999,999									N/C To:	99999999	
Dept From:	0											
Dept To:	999											

Tran No.	Type	Date	A/C Ref	N/C	Inv Ref	Dept.	Details	Net Amount	Tax Amount	T/C	Gross Amount	V	B
1	SI	10/06/2016	OC001	9998	10013	0	Opening Balance	2,904.20	0.00	T9	2,904.20	-	-
2	SI	17/06/2016	VH001	9998	10016	0	Opening Balance	9,900.78	0.00	T9	9,900.78	-	-
3	SI	24/06/2016	CS001	9998	10019	0	Opening Balance	5,726.88	0.00	T9	5,726.88	-	-
							Totals:	18,531.86	0.00		18,531.86		

He prints out a Day Books: Supplier Invoices (Detailed) report to check that supplier opening balance details are accurate following a similar pathway.

Date: Time:		**Tapper Timber** **Day Books: Supplier Invoices (Detailed)**									Page: 1	

Date From:	01/01/1980									Supplier From:		
Date To:	31/12/2019									Supplier To:	ZZZZZZZZ	
Transaction From:	1									N/C From:		
Transaction To:	99,999,999									N/C To:	99999999	
Dept From:	0											
Dept To:	999											

Tran No.	Type	Date	A/C Ref	N/C	Inv Ref	Dept	Details	Net Amount	Tax Amount	T/C	Gross Amount	V	B
4	PI	20/06/2016	CP001	9998	7611	0	Opening Balance	6,242.52	0.00	T9	6,242.52	-	-
5	PI	23/06/2016	ET001	9998	16-2408	0	Opening Balance	4,506.00	0.00	T9	4,506.00	-	-
6	PI	27/06/2016	JF001	9998	M41997	0	Opening Balance	5,006.82	0.00	T9	5,006.82	-	-
							Totals	15,755.34	0.00		15,755.34		

Lastly Ross prints out a trial balance. He does this by choosing NOMINAL CODES on the vertical toolbar and then clicking TRIAL BALANCE on the module toolbar. He chooses Preview and Run, and in Criteria Values he chooses July 2016 from the drop-down options.

A trial balance is a list of the account balances of the business. It shows the control (total) accounts as follows:

Debtors control account   £18,531.86

Creditors control account   £15,755.34

The suspense account has been created automatically and shows the arithmetic difference (£2,776.52) between the control accounts. It is put in automatically by the system to make the two columns balance.

Date:	**Tapper Timber**		Page: 1
Time:	**Period Trial Balance**		

To Period: Month 1, July 2016

N/C	Name	Debit	Credit
1100	Debtors Control Account	18,531.86	
2100	Creditors Control Account		15,755.34
9998	Suspense Account		2,776.52
	Totals:	18,531.86	18,531.86

The customer and supplier records are now complete and their account balances summarised in the two control accounts.

The trial balance is far from complete, however, and Ross's next task is to input the general ledger balances – eg inventory value, bank balance, loans, capital. When these items have been entered the trial balance should 'balance' – the two columns will have the same total and the suspense account will disappear.

AMENDING RECORDS

As well as setting up customer and supplier records, an organisation operating a computer accounting system will from time-to-time need to amend its records. For example:

- to take account of changes of address, contact names, terms of supply
- by indicating that the account is no longer active
- by deleting the account (if the system allows you to – see next page)

amending records in Sage

The procedures in Sage are very straightforward:

- select either CUSTOMERS or SUPPLIERS as appropriate
- highlight the record that needs amending, click EDIT and go to the
    - DETAILS screen (for customer or supplier details) or
    - CREDIT CONTROL screen (for terms of supply, eg credit limit)
- make the necessary change on-screen
- SAVE

In the example at the top of the next page, the name of a customer contact and email address at Oliver Cole & Sons has been changed from Jem Cole to Dan Cole.

In the example below, the credit limit of £10,000 given to customer Cornwood Stud has been increased to £15,000.

'closing' a customer or supplier account

The question may well arise "What should we do if a customer has ceased trading, or if we no longer use a particular supplier?" The logical answer is to close the account.

Sage does not allow you to **delete** an account when transactions have been recorded on it, even if the balance is nil. However, you can change the status of the account on the Credit Control screen in the customer record to 'Closed (On Hold)'.

If, on the other hand, the account has no transactions on it (eg it may have been opened and not used), it may be closed by clicking on the Delete icon on the toolbar. Here the account of Perry Builders can be deleted.

Click delete icon

							Refund	
Batch invoice	Batch credit	Customer receipt	Aged debt	Disputes	Price lists	Credit charges	Contra entries	Debt analysis	Write offs / Comms.	Delete

All records (4)			
	Inactive	Balance	Credit Limit	Contact
		5726.88	20000.00	Nicola Ashby
		2904.20	10000.00	Dan Cole
		0.00	5000.00	Doug Parry
		9900.78	20000.00	Sana Roy

Chapter Summary

■ Businesses buy and sell products either on a cash basis (immediate payment) or on credit (payment made later).

■ The accounting records for selling on credit comprise the accounts of customers (receivables/debtors) contained in the Sales Ledger.

■ The accounting records for buying on credit comprise the accounts of suppliers (payables/creditors) contained in the Purchases Ledger.

■ A business will also have to agree the terms of trading with a customer – the credit limit, the level of discount and the payment period it allows.

■ Setting up Customer and Supplier records involves the input of details such as names, addresses and outstanding financial transactions.

■ Records set up in this way should be carefully checked against printed out reports such as the Day Book Report and the trial balance.

■ Customer and Supplier records can also be amended or deleted (where allowable) as required.

Key Terms

cash sale	a sale where payment is immediate
credit sale	a sale where payment follows after an agreed period of time
receivables (debtors)	customers who owe money to a business
payables (creditors)	suppliers who are owed money by a business
debtors control account	the total of the balances of debtors' accounts
creditors control account	the total of the balances of creditors' accounts
credit terms	discounts and extended payment periods allowed to customers who make purchases
defaults	sets of data on the computer which are automatically applied

Activities

3.1   A cash sale is a sale where the only means of payment is notes and coins. True or false?

3.2   Define:

   (a)   a receivable (debtor)

   (b)   a payable (creditor)

3.3   What books of the business (ledgers) contain:

   (a)   receivables' (debtors') accounts

   (b)   payables' (creditors') accounts

3.4   What is shown in:

   (a)   Sales Ledger Control Account (known in Sage as Debtors Control Account)

   (b)   Purchases Ledger Control Account (known in Sage as Creditors Control Account)

3.5   What is the difference between a trade discount and a settlement discount?

3.6   What report shows the debit and credit balances of the accounts in an accounting system?

3.7   There are two important pieces of information (excluding financial transactions) that are missing from the computer-held customer details shown below. What are they, and why are they important?

Account name	John Butler & Associates
Address	24 Shaw Street
	Mereford
	MR4 6KJ
Contact name	John Butler

Telephone 01908 824342, Fax 01908 824295, Email mail@jbutler.co.uk

3.8   Can you delete a customer or supplier record in Sage if you cease to deal with the customer or supplier?

TAPPER TIMBER INPUTTING TASKS

> **warning note!**
> This activity involves you in setting up Customer and Supplier records in Sage and inputting live data into the computer.
> Ensure that you have changed your program date to 1 July 2016 in SETTINGS.
>
> Also check that the Customer and Supplier Defaults are set to Nominal codes 4000 and 5000 respectively. The default tax code should be T1 (standard rate). The Customer Trading terms in Configuration Editor can also be set up for payment due days as 30 days and terms of payment 30 days of invoice.

Task 1

Enter the customer details into the Customers screens as indicated in the Case Study.

The three customer records are as follows:

Account reference: OC001
Oliver Cole & Sons
Wood Farm
Collingwood
ST8 6TF
Contact name: Jem Cole
Telephone: 01908 824295
Email: jem@olivercole.co.uk
Credit limit: £5,000
Invoice 10013, 10 June 2016, £2904.20

Account reference: VH001
Victoria Hotel
67 The Parade
Stourcastle
ST4 6HG
Contact name: Sana Roy
Telephone: 01908 345287
Email: mail@victoriahotel.com
Credit limit: £15,000
Invoice 10016, 17 June 2016, £9,900.78

Account reference: CS001

Cornwood Stud

The Foal Yard

Bartisham

ST6 4KG

Contact name: Nicola Ashby

Telephone: 01908 674237

Email: ashby@cornwood.net

Credit limit: £10,000

Invoice 10019, 24 June 2016, £5,726.88

Task 2

Enter the supplier details into the Suppliers screens as indicated in the Case Study.

The three supplier records are as follows:

Account reference: CP001

Chapman Panels

17 Main Street

Martleford

ST5 2BG

Contact name: Ella Chapman

Telephone: 01722 295611

Email: sales@chapmanpanels.co.uk

Credit limit: £15,000

Terms: Payment due 30 days

Invoice ref 7611, 20 June 2016, £6,242.52

Account reference: ET001

Estate Timber Ltd

Woodbury Farm

Martleford

ST5 5FG

Contact name: Brian Cope

Telephone: 01722 628161

Email: info@estatetimber.com

Credit limit: £7,500

Terms: Payment due 30 days

Invoice ref 16-2408, 23 June 2016, £4,506.00

Account reference: JF001

Johnsons Fixings

Unit 5

Huckle Estate

Stourcastle

ST4 7SL

Contact name: Mack Pang

Telephone: 01908 949233

Email: johnsons@fixings.com

Credit limit: £15,000

Terms: Payment due 30 days

Invoice M41997, 27 June 2016, £5,006.82

Task 3

Print out a Day Books: Customer Invoices (Detailed) report for the new Customer accounts and check and agree the amounts you have input. Check it against the printout on page 183.

Task 4

Print out a Day Books: Supplier Invoices (Detailed) report for the new Supplier accounts and check and agree the amounts you have input. Check it against the printout on page 183.

Task 5

Print out a trial balance for July 2016 and check that the Debtors and Creditors Control account balances agree with the figures on page 47 and the totals shown on the Day Book reports produced in Tasks 3 and 4.

Task 6

Jem Cole, who is your named contact at Oliver Cole & Sons, retires. He has been replaced by Dan Cole. His email address is dan@olivercole.co.uk. Amend the customer details as appropriate.

Task 7

At the beginning of July the credit limit for Cornwood Stud is increased to £15,000. Amend the customer record.

Reminder! Have you made a back-up?

4 Setting up the general ledger

this chapter covers...

■ *In the last two chapters we have set up the business and entered details of Customers and Suppliers. All that remains to be done is to set up the General or Nominal Ledger.*

■ *The General Ledger contains all the other accounts in the accounting system:*
  - *income accounts, including Sales*
  - *purchases accounts for goods that the business trades in*
  - *expenses and overheads accounts*
  - *asset accounts (for items the business owns)*
  - *liability accounts (for items the business owes)*
  - *capital accounts (the investment of the business owner)*

■ *The General Ledger lists the bank accounts of the business, but they are operated through a separate BANK ACCOUNTS module, just as in a manual accounting system the bank accounts are recorded in a Cash Book, kept separately from the General Ledger accounts.*

■ *The accounts in the General Ledger are set up using the structure of a 'Chart of Accounts' provided by the program. This allocates suitable reference numbers to the various accounts which are grouped in categories (eg expenses, assets, liabilities) so that the computer program knows where to find them in the system and can then provide suitable reports to management.*

■ *One of the reports produced by the computer is the trial balance, which lists the general ledger account balances in two balancing columns. When the balances of all the accounts have been entered on the computer, the two columns should balance and the Suspense Account (which records any difference) should disappear.*

GENERAL LEDGER ACCOUNTS

An account in an accounting system records financial transactions and provides a running balance of what is left in the account at the end of each day. The **general ledger**, also referred to as the nominal ledger, accounts are the accounts which are not Customer accounts (sales ledger) or Supplier accounts (purchases ledger). They record:

- income – eg sales, rent received
- expenses – eg wages, advertising
- assets – items that a business owns or amounts that it is owed
- liabilities – money that a business owes, eg loans or creditors
- capital – money invested by the owner(s) and profits made

bank accounts

In a manual accounting system the bank accounts are kept in a separate Cash Book. In Sage the bank accounts of the business are *listed* in NOMINAL CODES, but they are *operated* through a separate BANK ACCOUNTS module.

the default ledger accounts

When Ross in the Case Study sets up his business he chooses the set of ledger accounts automatically provided by the program.

If you click on the NOMINAL CODES option in the Sage opening screen the default accounts are shown when the LIST option is chosen. You can scroll down this screen to see the whole list (summarised on the next page).

Check the List option

N/C	Name	Debit	Credit
0010	Freehold Property		
0011	Leasehold Property		
0020	Plant and Machinery		
0021	Plant/Machinery Depreciation		
0030	Office Equipment		
0031	Office Equipment Depreciation		
0040	Furniture and Fixtures		
0041	Furniture/Fixture Depreciation		
0050	Motor Vehicles		
0051	Motor Vehicles Depreciation		
1001	Stock		
1002	Work in Progress		
1003	Finished Goods		
1004	Raw Materials		
1100	Debtors Control Account	18531.86	
1101	Sundry Debtors		
1102	Other Debtors		

Nominal Code List

0010	Freehold Property
0011	Leasehold Property
0020	Plant and Machinery
0021	Plant/Machinery Depreciation
0030	Office Equipment
0031	Office Equipment Depreciation
0040	Furniture and Fixtures
0041	Furniture/Fixture Dpn
0050	Motor Vehicles
0051	Motor Vehicles Depreciation
1001	Stock
1002	Work in Progress
1003	Finished Goods
1004	Raw materials
1100	Debtors Control Account
1101	Sundry Debtors
1102	Other Debtors
1103	Prepayments
1104	Inter-company Debtors
1105	Provision for Credit Notes
1106	Provision for Doubtful Debts
1200	Bank Current Account
1210	Bank Deposit Account
1220	Building Society Account
1230	Petty Cash
1235	Cash Register
1240	Company Credit Card
1250	Credit Card Receipts
2100	Creditors Control Account
2101	Sundry Creditors
2102	Other Creditors
2109	Accruals
2200	Sales Tax Control Account
2201	Purchase Tax Control Acc.
2202	VAT Liability
2204	Manual Adjustments
2210	P.A.Y.E.
2211	National Insurance
2220	Net Wages
2230	Pension Fund
2300	Loans
2310	Hire Purchase
2320	Corporation Tax
2330	Mortgages
3000	Capital
3010	Capital Introduced
3050	Drawings
3100	Reserves
3101	Undistributed Reserves
3200	Profit and Loss Account
4000	Sales Type A
4001	Sales Type B
4002	Sales Type C
4009	Discounts Allowed
4010	Mgmt Charges Receivable
4099	Flat Rate – Benefit/Cost
4100	Sales Type D
4101	Sales Type E
4200	Sales of Assets
4400	Credit Charges (Late P'ments)
4900	Miscellaneous Income
4901	Royalties Received
4902	Commissions Received
4903	Insurance Claims
4904	Rent Income
4905	Distribution and Carriage
5000	Materials Purchased
5001	Materials Imported
5002	Miscellaneous Purchases
5003	Packaging
5009	Discounts Taken
5100	Carriage
5101	Import Duty
5102	Transport Insurance
5200	Opening Stock
5201	Closing Stock
6000	Productive Labour
6001	Cost of Sales Labour
6002	Sub-Contractors
6100	Sales Commissions
6200	Sales Promotions
6201	Advertising
6202	Gifts and Samples
6203	P.R.(Literature & Brochures)
6900	Miscellaneous Expenses
7000	Gross Wages
7001	Directors Salaries
7002	Directors Remuneration
7003	Staff Salaries
7004	Wages-Regular
7005	Wages-Casual
7006	Employers N.I.
7007	Employers Pensions
7008	Recruitment Expenses
7009	Adjustments
7010	SSP Reclaimed
7011	SMP Reclaimed
7100	Rent
7102	Water Rates
7103	General Rates
7104	Premises Insurance
7200	Electricity
7201	Gas
7202	Oil
7203	Other Heating Costs
7300	Vehicle Fuel
7301	Vehicle Repairs & Servicing
7302	Vehicle Licences
7303	Vehicle Insurance
7304	Misc Motor Expenses
7305	Congestion Charges
7306	Mileage Claims
7350	Scale Charges
7400	Travelling
7401	Car Hire
7402	Hotels
7403	U.K. Entertainment
7404	Overseas Entertainment
7405	Overseas Travelling
7406	Subsistence
7500	Printing
7501	Postage and Carriage
7502	Office Stationery
7503	Books etc
7550	Telephone and Fax
7551	Internet Charges
7552	Computers and Software
7553	Mobile Charges
7600	Legal Fees
7601	Audit Fees
7602	Accountancy Fees
7603	Consultancy Fees
7604	Professional Fees
7605	Mgt Charges Payable
7606	Software Subscriptions
7700	Equipment Hire
7701	Office Machine Maintenance
7702	Equipment Leasing
7703	Leasing Costs
7800	Repairs and Renewals
7801	Cleaning
7802	Laundry
7803	Premises Expenses
7900	Bank Interest Paid
7901	Bank Charges
7902	Currency Charges
7903	Loan Interest Paid
7904	H.P. Interest
7905	Credit Charges
7906	Exchange Rate Variance
7907	Other Interest Charges
7908	Factoring Charges
8000	Depreciation
8001	Plant/Machinery Depreciation
8002	Furniture/Fitting Depreciation
8003	Vehicle Depreciation
8004	Office Equipment Dpn
8100	Bad Debt Write Off
8102	Bad Debt Provision
8200	Donations
8201	Subscriptions
8202	Clothing Costs
8203	Training Costs
8204	Insurance
8205	Refreshments
8206	Cash Register Discrepancies
8250	Sundry Expenses
9001	Taxation
9998	Suspense Account
9999	Mispostings Account

CHART OF ACCOUNTS

If you look at the nominal code list you will see that a four digit code is given to each account in the general ledger. These account number codes range from 0010 to 9999. Ross is very unlikely to use all these accounts and may even want to change some.

What is important, however, is that any user of computerised accounting understands that these accounts are organised into categories by account number. These categories are set out in the **chart of accounts.** They can be accessed in the NOMINAL CODES screen by clicking on the CHART OF ACCOUNTS icon and then EDIT:

The left hand panel shows the **categories** of account, eg Sales, Purchases. If you click on a category you will see the ranges of accounts and account numbers covered by that category displayed below and in the right-hand panel.

In this case the Sales category has been selected and the types of Sales listed below. This panel tells you that all Product Sales should have an account number between 4000 and 4099. When you set up the Customer records in the previous chapter you chose 4000 as the default number (see page 40) for sales to customers.

But if you wanted to categorise customer sales (by area or type of product, for example) you could choose to have three accounts running for Product Sales: 4000 Sales Type A, 4001 Sales Type B, 4002 Sales Type C.

reports from Nominal Codes list

The general ledger accounts are used as the basis for a number of computer-generated management reports telling the owner about subjects such as the profit and the value of the business. If accounts get into the wrong category, the reports will also be wrong.

a summary of categories

It may be that a new business will adopt all the default nominal accounts (see list on page 58) because it does not need any others, but if a new account has to be set up it is critical that the new account is in the right category. The business owner will therefore need to understand what the categories mean and what they include.

The nominal code categories and account number ranges are:

Sales	4000 - 4999	income from sales of goods or services
Purchases	5000 - 5299	items bought to produce goods to sell
Direct Expenses	6000 - 6999	expenses directly related to producing goods
Overheads	7000 - 8299	expenses the business has to pay anyway
Taxation	9001 - 9001	corporation tax due on company profits

These are used to produce the **income statement (profit and loss account)** *which shows what profit (or loss) the business has made.*

Fixed Assets	0010 - 0059	items bought to keep in the business long-term
Current Assets	1000 - 1250	items owned by the business in the short-term
Current Liabilities	2100 - 2299	items owed by the business in the short-term
Long Term Liabilities	2300 - 2399	items owed by the business in the long-term
Capital & Reserves	3000 - 3299	the financial investment of the owner(s)

These are used to produce the **statement of financial position (balance sheet)** *which gives an idea of the value of the business and shows the owner what is represented by the capital investment (the money put in by the owner).*

Note that **Fixed Assets** *are also known by the international term of* **Non-current Assets**.

We will now put this theory into practice with a continuation of the Tapper Timber Case Study.

TAPPER TIMBER:
SETTING UP THE LEDGER ACCOUNTS

Ross's general ledger balances as at 1 July 2016 have been brought forward from his manual bookkeeping system.

financing

£25,000 of Ross's own money and retained profits are invested in the business.

Assets

The accounts show the following assets:

Plant and machinery	£15,490.00
Office equipment	£10,965.00
Inventory	£18,467.18
Debtors	£18,531.86
Bank	£13,210.58
Cash	£34.68

Liabilities

The accounts show the following liabilities:

Creditors	£15,755.34	
VAT	£4,640.16	(Sales tax less purchases tax)
Bank loan	£31,303.80	
Capital	£25,000.00	

Trial balance as at 1 July 2016

	Dr £	Cr £
Plant & Machinery	15,490.00	
Office Equipment	10,965.00	
Inventory	18,467.18	
Debtors Control	18,531.86	
Bank	13,210.58	
Cash	34.68	
Creditors Control		15,755.34
Sales Tax Control		12,710.26
Purchases Tax Control	8,070.10	
Bank loan		31,303.80
Capital		25,000.00
Totals	84,769.40	84,769.40

Tapper Timber trial balance (on the previous page)

The balances are listed as a trial balance. The columns are headed up Debit (Dr) and Credit (Cr) and they show the same total. A trial balance shows:

- Debits = assets and expenses
- Credits = liabilities, capital and income
- The amount owed by customers is shown in the Debtors Control account. It is a debit balance (an asset of the business).
- The amount owed to suppliers is shown in the Creditors Control account. It is a credit balance (a liability of the business).
- Tapper Timber is registered with HMRC for VAT. The VAT registration number must be shown on sales invoices. This means the business must charge VAT on sales. Sales VAT is owed to HMRC and is shown in the Sales Tax Control Account as a credit. VAT charged by suppliers on purchases can be reclaimed and is shown in the Purchase Tax Control Account as a debit. The balance owed to HMRC is the difference between the two account balances. In this case it is the balance of the Sales Tax Control Account balance (£12,710.26) less the balance of the Purchase Tax Control Account (£8,070.10) = £4,640.16

inputting the account balances

The date is 1 July 2016. Ross uses the trial balance form as a source document for inputting the nominal code balances as follows:

1 He clicks on the NOMINAL CODES option on the vertical toolbar and chooses the LIST view. He looks at the Nominal codes list which appears on the screen. He allocates account numbers to his account balances as follows:

Plant & Machinery	0020
Office Equipment	0030
Inventory	1001
Debtors Control	1100
Bank	1200
Cash	1230
Creditors Control	2100
Sales Tax Control	2200
Purchase Tax Control	2201
Bank loan	2300
Capital	3000

2 Ross scrolls down the screen and clicks on all the accounts that he is going to need while holding down the CTRL key – they then show as selected. Importantly he does not click on the following two accounts:
- Debtors control
- Creditors control

This is because he has already input Customer (Debtor) and Supplier (Creditor) balances (see the previous chapter). If he inputs these totals again they will be entered twice and will cause an imbalance.

The NOMINAL CODES screen is shown below.

3. Ross is now ready to input the balance values of the selected accounts. To do this he selects the EDIT icon which brings up a record window. He clicks on O/B in the balance box which opens a setup window. The date defaults to 1 July 2016 if he has set the program date correctly. The balance must go in the correct box – debits on the left, credits on the right. The first entry will look like the one shown below.

N/C*	0020
Name	Plant and Machinery
Balance	0.00	Account Type	Nominal Account

Month	Actuals	Budgets	To end Jun 2016
B/F	0.00	0.00	0.00
Jul	0.00	0.00	0.00
Aug	0.00	0.00	0.00
Sep	0.00	0.00	0.00
Oct			0.00
Nov			0.00
Dec			0.00
Jan			0.00
Feb			0.00
Mar			0.00
Apr	0.00	0.00	0.00
May	0.00	0.00	0.00
Jun	0.00	0.00	0.00
Future	0.00	0.00	0.00
Total	0.00	0.00	0.00

Opening Balance Setup

Ref	Date	Debit	Credit
O/Bal	01/07/2016	15490.00	0.00

Save   Cancel

The record is then saved. Ross will repeat this for all the selected accounts and their balance values. He can use the arrow button at the bottom of the screen to move from one record to the next.

As an alternative to selecting all the accounts at once, he could open each account in turn and enter the opening balances.

checking the input

Ross should check that what he has input is accurate. He can check his original list of balances against the computer's trial balance by printing a Trial Balance report.

This is produced by clicking on the TRIAL BALANCE icon within the NOMINAL CODES screen. The report is shown below.

Date: Time:		Tapper Timber Period Trial Balance		Page: 1
To Period:	Month 1, July 2016			
N/C	**Name**		**Debit**	**Credit**
0020	Plant and Machinery		15,490.00	
0030	Office Equipment		10,965.00	
1001	Stock		18,467.18	
1100	Debtors Control Account		18,531.86	
1200	Bank Current Account		13,210.58	
1230	Petty Cash		34.68	
2100	Creditors Control Account			15,755.34
2200	Sales Tax Control Account			12,710.26
2201	Purchase Tax Control Account		8,070.10	
2300	Loans			31,303.80
3000	Capital			25,000.00
		Totals:	84,769.40	84,769.40

Is the input correct? Yes. All the figures agree with the original (manual) trial balance figures and they are all in the correct column. The totals also agree.

You will see that the Suspense Account, which the system created in the previous chapter (see page 47), has now disappeared because the total of the debits now equals the total of the credits, as on Ross's original trial balance.

Ross is now ready to input July's transactions: new sales and purchase invoices and new payments in and out of the bank. These will be dealt with in the chapters that follow.

CHANGING AND ADDING GENERAL ACCOUNT NAMES

It is possible to change the names of accounts in the General Ledger if they do not fit in with the nature of your business. If, for example, you run a travel agency some account names may be very different from the names used by an insurance broker.

Accounts can be added to the General Ledger. Care should be taken to ensure that any new account fits into the Chart of Accounts structure (see page 59).

In the Case Study continuation on the next page, Ross changes the names of his Sales accounts to reflect more accurately what is going on in his business. He also plans to add Animal housing to his sales accounts. Coding of purchases for resale could be changed or expanded to categorise purchases, but Ross considers the default Materials Purchased code of 5000 sufficient for his purposes.

TAPPER TIMBER:
CHANGING AND ADDING NOMINAL ACCOUNTS

Ross looks at the list of account names on-screen and realises that the default Sales accounts are named Type A, Type B and Type C. This does not make clear what he has sold in each of his categories of sales – Fencing, Garden furniture and Sheds - so he decides to change the names as follows:

Account number	Old name	New name
4000	Sales Type A	Sales - Fencing
4001	Sales Type B	Sales - Garden furniture
4002	Sales Type C	Sales - Sheds

He selects the three accounts in the NOMINAL CODES list screen, goes to EDIT and overwrites the old name in the name box for each account and Saves. The amended screen for Account 4000 (Sales - Fencing) is shown below.

Ross has recently added a new sales category – Animal housing – to cover the sale of items such as kennels, hutches and coops. To add a new nominal account, Ross clicks on NEW and types 4003 into the N/C box. Sage recognises this as a New Account.

He enters Sales - Animal housing in the account name box. There is no opening balance so Ross saves the new record. This account will now appear in the nominal code list.

Ross now prints a Nominal List from REPORTS in NOMINAL CODES under Nominal Details. This shows all the accounts available to the business including his new customised accounts.

Date: Time:	**Tapper Timber** **Nominal List**	Page: 1

N/C From:
N/C To: 99999999

N/C	Name
0010	Freehold Property
0011	Leasehold Property
0020	Plant and Machinery
0021	Plant/Machinery Depreciation
0030	Office Equipment
0031	Office Equipment Depreciation
0040	Furniture and Fixtures
0041	Furniture/Fixture Depreciation
0050	Motor Vehicles
0051	Motor Vehicles Depreciation
1001	Stock
1002	Work in Progress
1003	Finished Goods
1004	Raw Materials
1100	Debtors Control Account
1101	Sundry Debtors
1102	Other Debtors
1103	Prepayments
1104	Inter-company Debtors
1105	Provision for credit notes
1106	Provision for doubtful debts
1200	Bank Current Account
1210	Bank Deposit Account
1220	Building Society Account
1230	Petty Cash
1235	Cash Register
1240	Company Credit Card
1250	Credit Card Receipts
2100	Creditors Control Account
2101	Sundry Creditors
2102	Other Creditors
2109	Accruals
2200	Sales Tax Control Account
2201	Purchase Tax Control Account
2202	VAT Liability
2204	Manual Adjustments
2210	P.A.Y.E.
2211	National Insurance
2220	Net Wages
2230	Pension Fund
2300	Loans
2310	Hire Purchase
2320	Corporation Tax
2330	Mortgages
3000	Capital
3010	Capital Introduced
3050	Drawings
3100	Reserves
3101	Undistributed Reserves
3200	Profit and Loss Account
4000	Sales - Fencing
4001	Sales - Garden furniture
4002	Sales - Sheds
4003	Sales - Animal housing
4009	Discounts Allowed

Chapter Summary

■ When a business sets up its accounts in a computer accounting package it will normally set up its Customer and Supplier records first.

■ The next stage will be for the business to set up its Ledger Accounts, adopting the default list of accounts supplied by the software in its 'Chart of Accounts' structure.

■ If the business has already started trading it should input all its Nominal Code Account balances (except for the Debtors and Creditors control accounts).

■ The input balances should be checked carefully against the source figures. The program can produce a trial balance which will show the balances that have been input.

■ Account names can be changed and new accounts added to suit the nature of the business – but it is important that the type of account should be consistent with the appropriate category in the 'Chart of Accounts'.

Key Terms

general ledger	the remaining accounts in the accounting system which are not Customers or Suppliers, eg income, expenses, assets, liabilities – also known as 'Nominal' ledger
chart of accounts	the structure of the nominal accounts, which groups accounts into categories such as Sales, Purchases, Overheads etc
categories	subdivisions of the Chart of Accounts (eg Sales, Purchases) each of which is allocated a range of account numbers by the computer
trial balance	a list of the accounts of a business divided into two columns: *debits* – mostly assets and expenses *credits* – mostly income and liabilities The two columns should have the same total, reflecting the workings of the double-entry bookkeeping system

Activities

4.1   Explain briefly what a Chart of Accounts is.

4.2   List the categories of account in a Chart of Accounts and write a sentence for each category, explaining what type of account that category includes.

4.3   You are transferring the manual accounting records of a company into a Sage system. The account names listed below are included in those used in the manual system. Refer to the Nominal Account list on page 58 and the categories of account numbers on page 60.

(a)   What account numbers will you allocate to these accounts?

(b)   In what categories in the Chart of Accounts will these accounts appear?

Complete the table below (or draw up your own table).

Account name	Account number	Category
Freehold Property		
Office Equipment		
Motor Vehicles		
Materials Purchased		
Bank Current Account		
Creditors Control		
Directors Salaries		
Electricity		
Capital		

TAPPER TIMBER INPUTTING TASKS

> **Warning note!**
> This activity involves inputting data into the computer.
> Remember to Save your data and keep your printouts as you progress through the tasks.

Task 1

Make sure the program date is set to 1 July 2016.

Open up the General Ledger and select accounts in the Nominal codes screen (list view) for the accounts included in the trial balance (see page 61).

But do *not* select Debtors Control Account or Creditors Control Account as they already have balances on them.

Task 2

Enter the balances from the trial balance (see page 61) into the appropriate General Ledger accounts as opening balances – but do not input the Debtors Control Account and the Creditors Control Account.

Make sure that debits and credits are entered correctly.

Task 3

Print out a trial balance for July 2016 from the computer and check it against the trial balance on page 64 and page 184, or have it checked by your tutor. The suspense account should have disappeared.

Task 4

Change the names of the three sales accounts as follows:

Number	Old name	New name
4000	Sales Type A	Sales - Fencing
4001	Sales Type B	Sales - Garden Furniture
4002	Sales Type C	Sales - Sheds

Task 5

Add new account number 4003 Sales - Animal housing to the Nominal code list.

Task 6

Print a Nominal List showing all accounts. Check the amended account names against the detail on page 66 of the Case Study.

Reminder! Have you made a back-up?

5 Selling to customers on credit

this chapter covers...

- *A business that sells on credit will invoice the goods or services supplied and then receive payment at a later date.*

- *The invoice is an important document because it sets out the details of the goods or services supplied, the amount owing, and the date by which payment should be made.*

- *Details of the invoice are entered in the computer accounting records so that the sale is recorded and the amount owed by the customer noted in the accounting system.*

- *A business that sells on credit may have to issue a refund for some or all of the goods or services supplied. They may be faulty or the sale may be cancelled. As payment has not yet been made, the 'refund' takes the form of a deduction from the amount owing. The document that the seller issues in this case is a credit note.*

- *A credit note is dealt with by a computer accounting program in much the same way as an invoice.*

- *This chapter continues the Tapper Timber Case Study and shows how details of invoices and credit notes are entered into the computer accounting records.*

BACKGROUND TO FINANCIAL DOCUMENTS

When a business sells goods or services it will use a number of different financial documents. A single sales transaction involves both seller and buyer. In this chapter we look at the situation from the point of view of the seller of the goods or services. Documents which are often used in the selling process for goods include:

■ **purchase order** which the seller receives from the buyer

■ **delivery note** which goes with the goods from the seller to the buyer

■ **invoice** which lists the goods and tells the buyer what is owed

■ **credit note** which is sent to the buyer if any refund is due

■ **statement** sent by the seller to remind the buyer what is owed

■ **remittance advice** sent by the buyer with the payment

Study the diagram below which shows how the documents 'flow' between buyer and seller.

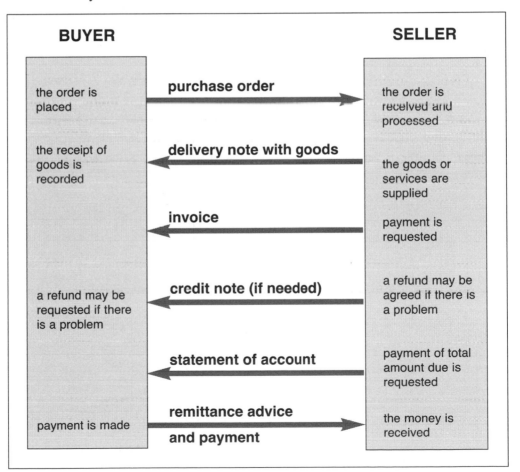

INVOICE

The main document we will deal with in this chapter is the **invoice** which is sent by the seller to the buyer to state what is owing and when it has to be paid. An invoice is illustrated below and explained on the next page.

INVOICE

Tapper Timber

Unit 3, Greenslade Way, Stourcastle, ST4 6TG
Telephone 01877 453611 Email: accounts@tappertimber.co.uk Web: www.tapper-timber.co.uk
VAT Reg GB 404 7106 52

invoice to

Victoria Hotel 67 The Parade Stourcastle ST4 6HG	

invoice no	**10023**
account	**VH001**
your reference	**47609**
date	**04 07 16**

product code	description	quantity	price	unit	total	discount %	net
GF09	Picnic tables	12	200.00	each	2,400.00	0%	2,400.00

goods total		2,400.00
VAT		480.00
TOTAL		2,880.00

terms
30 days

The invoice here has been issued by Tapper Timber for picnic tables ordered by Victoria Hotel on purchase order number 47609.

The reference number quoted here is the order number on Victoria Hotel's original purchase order.

The date here is the date on which the goods have been sent. It is known as the 'invoice date'.

The date is important for calculating when the invoice is due to be paid. In this case the 'terms' (see the bottom left-hand corner of the invoice) are 30 days. This means the invoice is due to be paid within 30 days of the invoice date.

The arithmetic and details in this line must be checked very carefully by Tapper Timber to make sure that they charge the correct amount:

- *product code* – this is the code for the picnic tables supplied
- *description* – this describes the goods ordered – the picnic tables
- *quantity* – this should be the same as the quantity on the purchase order
- *price* – this is the price of each unit shown in the next column
- *unit* is the way in which the item is charged, eg each (single items), or 10s, or boxes
- *total* is the price multiplied by the quantity
- *discount %* is the percentage allowance (known as trade discount) given to customers who regularly deal with the supplier or for high-value sales, ie a certain percentage (eg 10%) is deducted from their bill. Here there is no discount.
- *net* is the amount due to the seller after deduction of trade discount, and before VAT is added on

The Goods Total is the total of the column above it. It is the final amount due to the seller before VAT is added on.

Value Added Tax (VAT) is calculated and added on – here it is 20% of the Goods Total, ie $£2,400.00 \times \dfrac{20}{100} = £480.00$

The VAT is then added to the Goods Total to produce the actual amount owing: $£2,400.00 + £480.00 = £2,880.00$

The 'terms' explain the conditions on which the goods are supplied. Here '30 days' means that Victoria Hotel has to pay within 30 days of 4 July.

CREDIT NOTE

The other document we will deal with in this chapter is the **credit note**.

The **credit note** is issued when some form of refund has to be given to the buyer of goods or services. This may happen as a result of non-delivery, damaged or faulty goods, return of goods or because of an overcharge. As payment has not yet been made the credit note allows the buyer to deduct an amount from the invoice when settlement is finally made.

Note that it is never acceptable practice to change the amounts on an invoice; a credit note is always required.

The credit note illustrated below has been issued by Tapper Timber because one of the picnic tables was missing from the delivery.

Study the document below and read the notes which follow.

CREDIT NOTE

Tapper Timber

Unit 3, Greenslade Way, Stourcastle, ST4 6TG
Telephone 01877 453611 Email: accounts@tappertimber.co.uk Web: www.tapper-timber.co.uk
VAT Reg GB 404 7106 52

to

Victoria Hotel		
67 The Parade		
Stourcastle		
ST4 6HG		

credit note no	551
account	VH001
your reference	47609
our invoice	10023
date/tax point	05 07 16

product code	description	quantity	price	unit	total	discount %	net
GF09	Picnic tables	1	200.00	each	200.00	0%	200.00

Reason for credit
Item missing from delivery.

GOODS TOTAL	200.00
VAT	40.00
TOTAL	240.00

notes on the credit note

You will see from the credit note on the previous page that the total is £240. This can be deducted from the invoice total (see page 72) of £2,880. In other words, Victoria Hotel now owes £2,880 minus £240 = £2,640.

Note in particular from the credit note opposite:

- The format of the credit note is very much the same as the invoice.

- Victoria Hotel's original purchase order number is shown – 47609.

- Tapper Timber's invoice number for the goods credited is shown – 10023.

- The columns (eg 'product code') are identical to those used on the invoice and work in exactly the same way.

- VAT is also included – it has to be refunded because the goods have not now been supplied.

- If there was any discount this should also be taken into account – but there is no discount here.

- The reason for the credit note (the 'reason for credit') is stated at the bottom of the document. Here it states that the item was missing from the delivery.

INVOICES, CREDIT NOTES AND SAGE

the bookkeeping background

Invoices and credit notes are entered into the accounting records of a business. They record the sales and refunds made to customers who have bought on credit – the **receivables (debtors)** of the business. The amounts from these documents combine to provide the total of the **Sales Ledger**, which is the section of the accounting records which contains all the customer balances. This is recorded in the **Debtors Control Account** which tells the business how much in total is owing from customers who have bought on credit.

methods of recording invoices and credit notes

When a business uses accounting software, it will have to make sure that the details of each invoice and credit note issued are entered into the computer accounting records.

batch entry

Details of invoices produced independently of the computer accounting program are entered on a **batch invoice** screen. A 'batch' is simply a group of items (eg a 'batch' of cakes in the oven). The term is used in this context to describe a group of invoices which are all input at one time. This may not be the day that each invoice is produced – it may be the end of the week, or even the month.

It is normal practice to add up the total value of the invoices that are being input – the 'batch total' – and check this total against the invoice total calculated by the computer from the actual input. This will pick up any errors.

A batch invoice entry screen with three invoices input is shown below.

notes on the data entry columns:

- 'A/C' column contains the customer account reference
- 'Date' is the date on which each invoice was issued
- 'Ref' column is the invoice number (note that they are consecutive)
- 'Ex.Ref' is optional – it could be used for the purchase order number
- 'N/C' column is the Nominal Account code which specifies which type of sale is involved
- 'Dept'* is 0 by default and is not used here
- 'Project Ref'* is optional and is not used here
  *These can be used to identify invoice values belonging to different departments or projects if required.
- 'Details' describes the goods that have been sold

■ 'Net' is the amount of the invoice before VAT is added on

■ 'T/C' is the tax code which sets up the VAT rate that applies – here T1 refers to Standard Rate VAT, and is the default rate set up in Customer Defaults in SETTINGS

■ 'VAT' is calculated automatically and posted to the Sales Tax Control Account

When the operator has completed the input and checked the batch totals with the computer totals, the batched entry can be saved.

computer printed invoices

Most accounting programs include a sales invoice production function. Invoices can be printed out or emailed direct to customers.

---

important note: treatment of invoicing in this book

In this book we will concentrate on the batch entry method of recording invoices and credit notes.

Case Study

TAPPER TIMBER:
PROCESSING SALES INVOICES AND CREDIT NOTES

Tapper Timber supplies timber products. At the beginning of July Ross Tapper input his General Ledger account balances and his Customer and Supplier details and balances into the accounting system. He has set up four Sales Accounts in his Nominal code list:

New name	Account number
Sales - Fencing	4000
Sales - Garden Furniture	4001
Sales - Sheds	4002
Sales - Animal housing	4003

It is now July 8th. Ross needs to input:

• Sales invoices issued to his customers

• Credit notes issued to his customers

SALES INVOICES ISSUED

Invoice	Name	Date	Details	Net amount £	VAT £
10023	Victoria Hotel	04/07/16	Garden furniture	2,400.00	480.00
10024	Oliver Cole & Sons	05/07/16	Stock fencing	658.25	131.65
10025	Cornwood Stud	07/07/16	Tack shed	5,740.00	1,148.00
Subtotals				8,798.25	1,759.65
Batch total					10,557.90

CREDIT NOTES ISSUED

Cr note	Name	Date	Details	Net amount £	VAT £
551	Victoria Hotel	05/07/16	Garden furniture missing	200.00	40.00
552	Oliver Cole & Sons	07/07/16	Stock fencing damaged	131.65	26.33
Subtotals				331.65	66.33
Batch total					397.98

batch invoice entry

Ross starts by opening the CUSTOMERS module and clicking on the BATCH INVOICE icon. This brings up the screen shown below. He will then:

- Identify the account reference code for each of the three customers

- Enter each invoice on a separate line

- Take the data from each invoice: date, invoice no. (Ref), product details and amounts

- Ignore the Dept and Project Ref columns

- Enter the appropriate Sales account number (N/C) for the type of sale

- Enter the T1 tax code for standard rate VAT and check that the VAT amount calculated on-screen is the same as on the invoice

When the input is complete Ross should check his original batch totals (net, VAT and total) against the computer totals. Once he is happy that his input is correct he hits SAVE.

Batch Customer Invoice

Clear form	Insert row (F7)	Remove row (F8)	Copy cell above (F6)	Copy cell above +1 (Shift + F6)	Calculate net (F9)	Memorise	Recall	Print list	Send to Excel

A/C Cornwood Stud

N/C Sales - Sheds

The batch total

Tax Rate 20.00

Total 10557.90

A/C*	Date*	Ref	Ex.Ref	N/C*	Department	Project Ref	Details	Net	T/C*	VAT
VH001	04/07/2016	10023		4001	0		Garden furn...	2400.00	T1	480.00
OC001	05/07/2016	10024		4000	0		Stock fencing	658.25	T1	131.65
CS001	07/07/2016	10025		4002	0		Tack shed	5740.00	T1	1148.00

The VAT total of the batch

The net total of the batch

8798.25   1759.65

Save   Close

checking the invoices are on the system

As a further check Ross prints out a Day Book report using the REPORTS icon on the CUSTOMERS toolbar. The title of the report is 'Day Books: Customer Invoices (Detailed)'. In the Criteria Values screen he enters a date range of 4 to 7 July. The report appears as follows:

Date:	**Tapper Timber**	**Page: 1**
Time:	**Day Books: Customer Invoices (Detailed)**	

Date From:	04/07/2016	**Customer From:**	
Date To:	07/07/2016	**Customer To:**	ZZZZZZZZ
Transaction From:	1	**N/C From:**	
Transaction To:	99,999,999	**N/C To:**	99999999
Dept From:	0		
Dept To:	999		

Tran No.	Type	Date	A/C Ref	N/C	Inv Ref	Dept.	Details	Net Amount	Tax Amount	T/C	Gross Amount	V	B
25	SI	04/07/2016	VH001	4001	10023	0	Garden furniture	2,400.00	480.00	T1	2,880.00	N	-
26	SI	05/07/2016	OC001	4000	10024	0	Stock fencing	658.25	131.65	T1	789.90	N	-
27	SI	07/07/2016	CS001	4002	10025	0	Tack shed	5,740.00	1,148.00	T1	6,888.00	N	-
							Totals:	8,798.25	1,759.65		10,557.90		

batch credit note entry

Ross enters the details of the two credit notes in much the same way as he processed the invoices. He starts by opening the CUSTOMERS screen but this time clicks on the BATCH CREDIT icon. This brings up the screen shown below. He identifies the account reference code for each of the two customers together with the correct Sales account number, and inputs the credit note details as shown below. When the input is complete he checks the batch totals agree. Once he is happy that his input is correct he hits SAVE.

Batch Customer Credit

Clear form | Insert row (F7) | Remove row (F8) | Copy cell above (F6) | Copy cell above +1 (Shift + F6) | Calculate net (F9) | Memorise | Recall | Print list | Send to Excel

A/C Oliver Cole & Sons
N/C Sales - Fencing

Tax Rate 20.00
Total 397.98

A/C*	Date*	Credit No	Ex.Ref	N/C*	Department	Project Ref	Details	Net	T/C*	VAT
VH001	05/07/2016	551		4001	0		Garden furn...	200.00	T1	40.00
OC001	07/07/2016	552		4000	0		Stock fencin...	131.65	T1	26.33
								331.65		66.33

checking the credit notes are on the system

As a further check Ross prints out a Day Book report using the REPORTS icon on the CUSTOMERS toolbar. The title of the report is 'Day Books: Customer Credits (Detailed)'. In the Criteria Values screen he enters a date range of 5 to 7 July. The report appears as follows:

Date: **Tapper Timber**   **Page:** 1
Time: **Day Books: Customer Credits (Detailed)**

Date From:	05/07/2016		Customer From:	
Date To:	07/07/2016		Customer To:	ZZZZZZZZ
Transaction From:	1		N/C From:	
Transaction To:	99,999,999		N/C To:	99999999
Dept From:	0			
Dept To:	999			

Tran No.	Type	Date	A/C Ref	N/C	Inv Ref	Dept.	Details	Net Amount	Tax Amount	T/C	Gross Amount	V	B
28	SC	05/07/2016	VH001	4001	551	0	Garden furniture missing	200.00	40.00	T1	240.00	N	-
29	SC	07/07/2016	OC001	4000	552	0	Stock fencing damaged	131.65	26.33	T1	157.98	N	-
							Totals:	331.65	66.33		397.98		

Chapter Summary

- When a business sells on credit it will issue an invoice to the buyer. This sets out the amount owing and the date by which it has to be paid.

- When a business has to make a refund to a credit customer it will issue a credit note. This sets out the value by which the amount owing is reduced.

- Sales invoices and credit notes are part of the 'flow of documents' that occurs when a sale is made on credit. The full list is purchase order, delivery note, invoice, credit note, statement, and remittance advice. Not all of these will be used in every instance.

- The details of invoices and credit notes must be entered into the accounting records of a business. If a computer program is used the details will be input on-screen.

- In computerised accounting sales invoices and credit notes are either produced within the program or entered in batch form.

- It is essential to check the details of invoices and credit notes which have been input. This can be done by printing out a Day Book Report.

Key Terms

credit sale	a sale made where payment is due at a later date
receivables (debtors)	customers who owe money to a business
sales ledger	the part of the accounting system where the customer accounts are kept – it records the amounts that are owed to the business
purchase order	the financial document which requests the supply of goods or services and specifies exactly what is required
invoice	the financial document which sets out the details of the goods sold or services provided, the amount owing and the date by which the amount is due
credit note	the financial document which reduces the amount owing by the customer
batch	a group of documents, eg invoices or credit notes
batch entry	the input of a number of documents in a group

Activities

5.1 Place the following documents in the order in which they are likely to be used in a transaction in which goods are sold on credit.

statement

invoice

purchase order

delivery note

remittance advice

credit note

5.2 A delivery note will always be used in a sale made on credit. True or false?

5.3 A credit note will always be used in a sale made on credit. True or false?

5.4 List two important pieces of information that the invoice will provide to the purchaser of goods or services.

5.5 Give a definition of the 'receivables' (debtors) of a business.

5.6 Where in the accounting records of a business will the receivables' (debtors') balances be found?

5.7 What arithmetic checks should be made when inputting details of invoices and credit notes into a computer accounting system?

5.8 What details would you expect to enter when inputting details of each invoice into a computer accounting system?

5.9 What is the purpose of the tax code when inputting details of an invoice or credit note into a computer accounting system?

TAPPER TIMBER INPUTTING TASKS

Warning note!

This activity involves inputting data into the computer.

Remember to Save your data and keep your printouts as you progress through the tasks.

Task 1

Making sure that you have set the program date to 8 July 2016, enter the following invoice details into the computer. Check your totals before saving and print out a Day Books: Customer Invoices (Detailed) Report to confirm the data that you have saved. You can limit the transactions shown on the report by selecting the transaction date range in 'report criteria' (here 4 to 7 July). Check this report against the report on page 79.

SALES INVOICES ISSUED					
Invoice	**Name**	**Date**	**Details**	**Net amount £**	**VAT £**
10023	Victoria Hotel	04/07/16	Garden furniture	2,400.00	480.00
10024	Oliver Cole & Sons	05/07/16	Stock fencing	658.25	131.65
10025	Cornwood Stud	07/07/16	Tack shed	5,740.00	1,148.00
Subtotals				8,798.25	1,759.65
Batch total					10,557.90

Task 2

Enter the following credit note details into the computer. Check your totals before saving and print out a Day Books: Customer Credits (Detailed) Report, date range 5 to 7 July. Check this report against the report on page 80.

CREDIT NOTES ISSUED					
Cr note	**Name**	**Date**	**Details**	**Net amount £**	**VAT £**
551	Victoria Hotel	05/07/16	Garden furniture missing	200.00	40.00
552	Oliver Cole & Sons	07/07/16	Stock fencing damaged	131.65	26.33
Subtotals				331.65	66.33
Batch total					397.98

Task 3

It is now 15 July 2016. Change your program date setting. You have a further batch of invoices to process. Enter the details into the computer. Check your totals before saving and print out a Day Books: Customer Invoices (Detailed) Report (11 to 14 July) and check it against the report on page 184.

Invoice	Name	Date	Details	Net amount £	VAT £
10026	Cornwood Stud	11/07/16	Palisade fencing	2,028.00	405.60
10027	Oliver Cole & Sons	12/07/16	5-bar gates (fencing)	425.00	85.00
10028	Victoria Hotel	14/07/16	Kennels (animal housing)	1138.60	227.72
Subtotals				3,591.60	718.32
Batch total					4,309.92

Task 4

On the same date you have another credit note to process. Enter the details shown below. Check your totals before saving and print out a Day Books: Customer Credits (Detailed) Report (15 July only) to confirm the data that you have saved. Check your printout against the report on page 185.

Finally, print out a trial balance for July and check it against the trial balance on page 185.

Cr note	Name	Date	Details	Net amount £	VAT £
553	Cornwood Stud	15/07/16	Overcharged tack shed	140.00	28.00
Batch total					168.00

Reminder! Have you made a backup?

6 Buying from suppliers on credit

this chapter covers...

■ This chapter should be read in conjunction with the previous chapter 'Selling to customers on credit' as it represents 'the other side of the coin' – the invoice and the credit note as they are dealt with by the purchaser.

■ A business purchaser that buys on credit will receive an invoice for the goods or services supplied and will then have to pay at a later date.

■ Details of invoices and credit notes received are entered by the purchaser into the computer accounting records. In this way the total amount owing to the supplier is recorded in the accounting system.

■ This chapter continues the Tapper Timber Case Study and shows how details of invoices and credit notes received are entered into supplier accounts in the computer accounting records.

INVOICES AND CREDIT NOTES

Make sure that you are familiar with the two types of financial document we will be dealing with – the invoice and the credit note. Read the descriptions below and remind yourself of the 'flow of documents' by studying the diagram below.

invoice

The main document we will deal with in this chapter is the **invoice** which is sent by the seller to the buyer to state the amount that is owing and the date by which it has to be paid. See page 72 for an illustration.

credit note

The **credit note** is issued by the seller when some form of refund has to be given to the buyer of goods or services. As payment has not yet been made the credit note allows the buyer to deduct an amount from the invoice when settlement is finally made. See page 74 for an illustration.

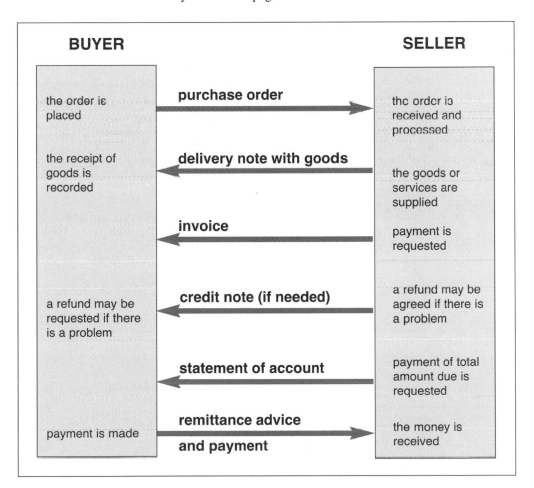

THE BOOKKEEPING BACKGROUND

Details of invoices and credit notes have to be entered into the accounting records of a business that buys on credit. They record the purchases made from suppliers – the **payables (creditors)** of the business.

The amounts from these documents combine to provide the total of the **Purchases Ledger**, the section of the accounting records which contains all the supplier accounts and their balances. The total of the **Purchases Ledger** (recorded in the **Creditors Control Account**) tells the business how much in total it owes to suppliers.

The documents received from the suppliers – invoices and credit notes – are recorded in the computer accounting system on the **batch** basis illustrated in the Case Study in the previous chapter. Documents received from a seller should be checked carefully and authorised before input.

PURCHASES AND EXPENSES AND CAPITAL ITEMS

One point that is very important to bear in mind is the difference between **purchases** and **expenses** and **capital items**, as it affects the Nominal Account codes used when inputting invoices and credit notes on the computer. Look at the Tapper Timber account list (with account numbers) shown below.

N/C	Name
0020	Plant and Machinery
0030	Office Equipment
0050	Motor Vehicles
1001	Stock
1100	Debtors Control Account
1200	Bank Current Account
1230	Petty Cash
2100	Creditors Control Account
2200	Sales Tax Control Account
2201	Purchase Tax Control Account
2300	Loans
3000	Capital
3050	Drawings
4000	Sales - Fencing
4001	Sales - Garden furniture
4002	Sales - Sheds
4003	Sales - Animal housing
5000	Materials Purchased
6201	Advertising
7550	Telephone and Fax
7700	Equipment Hire

Purchases are items a business buys which it expects to turn into a product or sell as part of its day-to-day business. For example:

■ a business that makes cheese will buy milk to make the cheese

■ a supermarket will buy food and consumer goods to sell to the public

All these items are bought because they will be sold or turned into a product that will be sold. In Sage these purchases will be recorded in a **purchases account**, normally 5000, or a number in that category. In the list shown on the previous page account 5000 is used for 'Materials Purchased'.

Expenses, on the other hand, are items which the business pays for which form part of the business running expenses (overheads), eg rent (7100) and electricity (7200). They all have separate Nominal Code numbers.

Capital items are 'one off' items that the business buys and intends to keep for a number of years, for example office equipment and furniture. These categories of asset all also have separate Nominal Code numbers in the range 0-0059.

Case Study

TAPPER TIMBER: PROCESSING PURCHASE INVOICES AND CREDIT NOTES

It is now 15 July 2016. Ross has a number of supplier invoices and supplier credit notes to enter into the computer accounting system.

He has grouped the documents into two batches.

PURCHASE INVOICES RECEIVED

Invoice	Name	Date	Details	Net amount £	VAT £
16-2941	Estate Timber	05/07/16	Posts and planks	1549.30	309.86
7655	Chapman Panels	11/07/16	Bow top panels	1230.00	246.00
M42206	Johnsons Fixings	12/07/16	Assorted fixings	391.25	78.25
Subtotals				3170.55	634.11
Batch total					3804.66

CREDIT NOTES RECEIVED

Cr note	Name	Date	Details	Net amount £	VAT £
R281	Johnsons Fixings	01/07/16	Post supports overcharged	136.00	27.20
C93	Chapman Panels	06/07/16	Returned hurdles	225.00	45.00
Subtotals				361.00	72.20
Batch total					433.20

batch invoice entry

Ross starts by opening up the SUPPLIERS screen and clicking on the BATCH INVOICE icon. This will show the screen below. He will then:

- Identify the account reference code for each of the three suppliers

- Enter each invoice on a separate line

- Take the data from the invoice: date, invoice no. (Ref), product details and amounts

- Ignore the Dept, Project Ref and Cost Code columns

- Enter the appropriate Materials Purchased account number 5000 under N/C

- Enter the T1 tax code for standard rate VAT and check that the VAT amount calculated on-screen is the same as on the invoice*

When the input is complete Ross checks his batch totals (Net, VAT, Total) against the computer totals. Once he is happy he hits SAVE.

*Sometimes the VAT on a document will vary by a penny or two from the VAT calculated on-screen. Any differences can be altered on-screen so that the VAT value entered agrees with the VAT on the document.

The batch suppliers' invoice screen will appear like this:

Batch Supplier Invoice — □ ×

Clear form | Insert row (F7) | Remove row (F8) | Copy cell above (F6) | Copy cell above +1 (Shift + F6) | Calculate net (F9) | Memorise | Recall | Print list | Send to Excel

A/C Johnsons Fixings

N/C Materials Purchased

The batch total

Tax Rate 20.00

Total 3804.66

A/C*	Date*	Ref	Ex.Ref	N/C*	Departmen	Project Ref	Cost Code	Details	Net	T/C*	VAT
ET001	05/07/2016	16-2941		5000	0			Posts and ...	1549.30	T1	309.86
CP001	11/07/2016	7655		5000	0			Bow top pa...	1230.00	T1	246.00
JF001	12/07/2016	M42206		5000	0			Assorted fi...	391.25	T1	78.25

The VAT total of the batch

The net total of the batch

3170.55 634.11

Save | Close

checking the invoices are on the system

As a further check Ross prints out a Day Book report using the REPORTS icon on the SUPPLIERS toolbar. The title of the report is 'Day Books: Supplier Invoices (Detailed)'. In the Criteria Values he enters a date range of 5 to 12 July. The report appears as follows:

Date:							Tapper Timber			Page:	1	
Time:							**Day Books: Supplier Invoices (Detailed)**					

Date From:	05/07/2016								Supplier From:			
Date To:	12/07/2016								Supplier To:	ZZZZZZZZ		

Transaction From:	1								N/C From:			
Transaction To:	99,999,999								N/C To:	99999999		

Dept From:	0
Dept To:	999

Tran No.	Type	Date	A/C Ref	N/C	Inv Ref	Dept	Details	Net Amount	Tax Amount	T/C	Gross Amount	V	B
34	PI	05/07/2016	ET001	5000	16-2941	0	Posts and planks	1,549.30	309.86	T1	1,859.16	N	-
35	PI	11/07/2016	CP001	5000	7655	0	Bow top panels	1,230.00	246.00	T1	1,476.00	N	-
36	PI	12/07/2016	JF001	5000	M42206	0	Assorted fixings	391.25	78.25	T1	469.50	N	-
							Totals	3,170.55	634.11		3,804.66		

batch credit note entry

Ross enters the details of the two credit notes in much the same way as he processed the invoices. He starts by opening the SUPPLIERS screen but this time clicks on the BATCH CREDIT icon. This brings up the screen shown below. He identifies the account reference code for each of the two suppliers and inputs the credit note details as shown below. He uses the Materials Purchased account number (5000). When the input is complete he checks the batch totals agree. Once he is happy that his input is correct he hits SAVE.

Batch Supplier Credit

Clear form | Insert row (F7) | Remove row (F8) | Copy cell above (F6) | Copy cell above +1 (Shift + F6) | Calculate net (F9) | Memorise | Recall | Print list | Send to Excel

A/C	Chapman Panels									Tax Rate		20.00
N/C	Materials Purchased									Total		433.20

A/C*	Date*	Credit No	Ex.Ref	N/C*	Departmen	Project Ref	Cost Code	Details	Net	T/C*	VAT
JF001	01/07/2016	R281		5000	0			Post suppo...	136.00	T1	27.20
CP001	06/07/2016	C93		5000	0			Returned h...	225.00	T1	45.00
									361.00		72.20

Save | Close

checking the credit notes are on the system

As a further check Ross prints out a Day Book report using the REPORTS icon on the SUPPLIERS toolbar. The title of the report is 'Day Books: Supplier Credits (Detailed)'. In the Criteria Values he enters a date range of 1 to 6 July. The report appears as follows:

Date:							Tapper Timber				Page:	1
Time:							**Day Books: Supplier Credits (Detailed)**					

Date From:	01/07/2016					Supplier From:	
Date To:	06/07/2016					Supplier To:	ZZZZZZZZ
Transaction From:	1					N/C From:	
Transaction To:	99,999,999					N/C To:	99999999
Dept From:	0						
Dept To:	999						

Tran No.	Type	Date	A/C Ref	N/C	Inv Ref	Dept	Details	Net Amount	Tax Amount	T/C	Gross Amount	V	B
37	PC	01/07/2016	JF001	5000	R281	0	Post supports	136.00	27.20	T1	163.20	N	-
38	PC	06/07/2016	CP001	5000	C93	0	Returned hurdles	225.00	45.00	T1	270.00	N	-
							Totals	361.00	72.20		433.20		

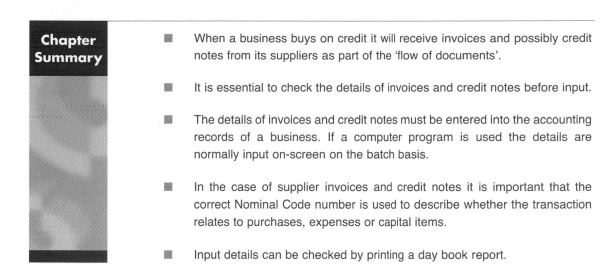

Chapter Summary

■ When a business buys on credit it will receive invoices and possibly credit notes from its suppliers as part of the 'flow of documents'.

■ It is essential to check the details of invoices and credit notes before input.

■ The details of invoices and credit notes must be entered into the accounting records of a business. If a computer program is used the details are normally input on-screen on the batch basis.

■ In the case of supplier invoices and credit notes it is important that the correct Nominal Code number is used to describe whether the transaction relates to purchases, expenses or capital items.

■ Input details can be checked by printing a day book report.

Key Terms

credit purchase	a purchase made where payment is due at a later date
payables (creditors)	suppliers to whom the business owes money
purchases ledger	the part of the accounting system where the suppliers' accounts are kept
purchases	items bought which will be turned into a product or be sold as part of day-to-day-trading
expenses	payments made which relate to the running of the business – also known as overheads
capital items	items bought which the business intends to keep
batch	a group of documents, eg invoices or credit notes

Activities

6.1 Define the term 'payables' (also known as 'creditors').

6.2 In what section of the accounting system are supplier balances kept? What information does this provide for the owner of the business?

6.3 What is the difference between purchases, expenses and capital items? Why is it important to identify these types of transaction before entering a supplier invoice on the computer?

6.4 Write a list of instructions for a person entering supplier invoices into a batch screen on a computer accounting program. Explain what data is entered in each of the columns and what checks should be made before and after input.

TAPPER TIMBER INPUTTING TASKS

Task 1

Set the program date to 15 July 2016. Enter the following invoice details into the computer. Check your totals before saving and print out a Day Books: Supplier Invoices (Detailed) Report, date range 5 to 12 July. Check this against the report on page 89.

PURCHASE INVOICES RECEIVED					
Invoice	**Name**	**Date**	**Details**	**Net amount £**	**VAT £**
16-2941	Estate Timber	05/07/16	Posts and planks	1549.30	309.86
7655	Chapman Panels	11/07/16	Bow top panels	1230.00	246.00
M42206	Johnsons Fixings	12/07/16	Assorted fixings	391.25	78.25
Subtotals				3170.55	634.11
Batch total					3804.66

Task 2

Enter the following credit note details into the computer. Check your totals before saving and print out a Day Books: Supplier Credits (Detailed) Report, date range 1 to 6 July. Check this against the report on page 90.

CREDIT NOTES RECEIVED					
Cr note	**Name**	**Date**	**Details**	**Net amount £**	**VAT £**
R281	Johnsons Fixings	01/07/16	Post supports overcharged	136.00	27.20
C93	Chapman Panels	06/07/16	Returned hurdles	225.00	45.00
Subtotals				361.00	72.20
Batch total					433.20

Task 3

Ross has received another supplier invoice. It is for some new machinery for use within the business. The invoice is shown below.

INVOICE

Emery Tools Ltd

Old Mill Works, Valley Road, Stourton, ST12 1SD

VAT reg GB 161 7035 29

invoice to

| Tapper Timber |
| Unit 3 Greenslade Way |
| Stourcastle |
| ST4 6TG |

invoice no	9241
account	ET002
your reference	2847
date	08 07 16

product code	description	quantity	price	unit	total	discount %	net
6072	Band saw	1	2000.00	each	2000.00	0	2000.00

terms
30 days

goods total	2,000.00
VAT	400.00
TOTAL	2,400.00

Enter new supplier details using account ref ET002, with a credit limit of £5,000 and 30 day terms. The supplier contact is Lorna Costelloe. Then enter the invoice details taking care to use the correct Nominal code (see the list on page 86).

When the input is complete, print out a Trial Balance for July 2016 and check it against the one shown on page 186.

Reminder! Have you made a back-up?

7 Customer and supplier payments

this chapter covers...

■ A computer accounting system includes more than one 'Bank' account in its General Ledger. We look at the range of accounts available.

■ This chapter focuses on the use of the bank current account for credit transactions, ie when a business receives payment of its customers' invoices and when it makes payment of its suppliers' invoices.

■ Customer and supplier payments are allocated to the transactions paid. Underpayments and overpayments can be recorded.

■ A remittance advice gives details of the payment.

THE BANK ACCOUNTS IN COMPUTER ACCOUNTING

The bank accounts and all the functions associated with them are found by clicking BANK ACCOUNTS on the vertical toolbar.

The BANK ACCOUNTS screen then appears as shown below.

Study the screen below and read the notes that follow. The most important icons are explained by the text with the arrows.

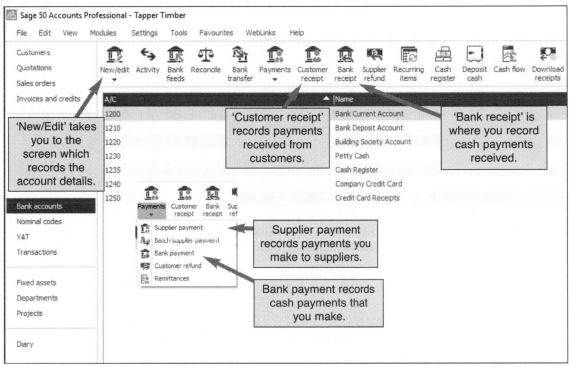

types of bank account

The accounts listed above come from the default list in the Chart of Accounts (see page 59 if you need reminding about this). The business does not have to adopt all the accounts listed here, but may use some of them if it needs them:

- **bank current account** records all payments in and out of the bank account used for everyday purposes – it is usually the most commonly used account

- **bank deposit account** and **Building Society account** can be used if the business maintains interest-paying accounts for savings and money that is not needed in the short term

- **petty cash account** can be used if the business keeps a petty cash supply in the office for small business purchases such as stationery and stamps
- **cash register** can be used to record takings in a retail business
- **company credit card account** can be used if the business issues credit cards to its employees to enable them to pay for expenses
- **credit card receipts account** can be used if the business receives credit or debit card payments from its customers

When a business is setting up its bank accounts it should click on NEW/EDIT on the BANK ACCOUNTS screen to open the bank account DETAILS screen:

This screen enables the business to input details of the account, the bank and bank contact and to see the activity on the account.

There may be a facility to connect directly to the bank via the internet and to obtain up-to-date transactions at any time.

RECORDING PAYMENTS FROM CUSTOMERS

how do payments arrive?

When a payment arrives from a customer who has bought on credit it can arrive at the business in a variety of ways:

- **Electronic bank transfer**. The Bankers Automated Clearing Services (BACS) system allows one party to pay another by electronic transfer of funds between bank accounts. The customer instructs his bank to pay the supplier's bank. The 'Faster Payments' service provides for same day transfers.

- **Cheque**. Although the use of cheques is diminishing, many small businesses still use them as a form of payment. A cheque is a written order, signed by the customer, to pay an amount to someone. Cheques must be physically paid into a bank; funds are then transferred after a 3-day clearing cycle has completed. Below is an example of a cheque payable to Tapper Timber from Victoria Hotel.

- **Cash**. Some small payments may still be made in person by cash.

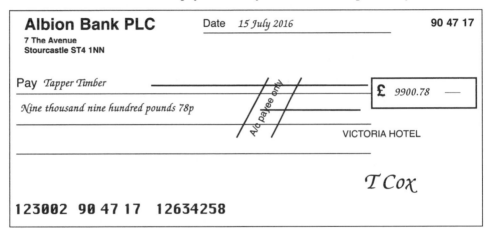

Customer payments are usually accompanied by a remittance advice – a document giving details of the payment. An example is shown below.

BACS REMITTANCE ADVICE		FROM: Oliver Cole & Sons Wood Farm Collingwood ST8 6TF
TO Tapper Timber Unit 3, Greenslade Way, Stourcastle, ST4 6TG		08 07 16
Your ref		Amount
10013	FASTER PAYMENT	2904.20
		TOTAL 2904.20

THIS HAS BEEN PAID BY BACS CREDIT TRANSFER DIRECTLY INTO YOUR BANK ACCOUNT AT ALBION BANK NO 11719881 SORT CODE 90 47 17

customer payments and the accounting system

An incoming payment from a customer settling one or more invoices (less any credit notes) needs to be recorded in the accounting system. The entry will:

- increase the balance in the bank account (a debit in double-entry)
- decrease the balance in the customer's account (and the Debtors Control Account) because the customer will owe less (a credit in double-entry accounting)

In computer accounting the payment is input once and the two entries will be automatically made from the same screen.

the practicalities

The business will normally input a number of payments at one time on a regular basis, eg every week, using the remittance advice and/or the bank statement as the source document.

The appropriate bank account should first be selected on the BANK ACCOUNTS screen and then the CUSTOMER RECEIPT icon selected to access the Customer Receipt input screen:

Customer Receipt - Bank Current Account

Clear form | Pay by card | Pay in full (F3) | Wizard | Automatic | Department | Print list | Send to Excel

Bank Details

Account Ref	1200
Name	Bank Current Account
Balance	16114.78

Customer Details

Account*	OC001
Name	Oliver Cole & Sons
Balance	1141.92

Receipt Details

Date*	08/07/2016
Amount	2904.20
Reference	FP receipt

The cheque amount

Show: All   From: / /   To: / /   ☐ List Invoice/Credit by item line

No.	Type	A/C	Date	Ref	Ex.Ref	Department	Details	T/C	Amount £	Disputed?	Receipt £	Discount £
1	SI	OC001	10/06/2016	10013		n/a	Opening Ba...	n/a	2904.20		2904.20	0.00
26	SI	OC001	05/07/2016	10024		n/a	Stock fencing	n/a	789.90		0.00	0.00
29	SC	OC001	07/07/2016	552		n/a	Stock fenci...	n/a	157.98		0.00	0.00
31	SI	OC001	12/07/2016	10027		n/a	5-bar gates	n/a	510.00		0.00	0.00

The cheque amount is allocated

The running total of the allocated amount

Analysis Total   2904.20

Save   Close

processing the payments received

The procedure for recording the customer payment on this screen is to:

- input the customer account reference – this will bring up on screen the account name and all the outstanding amounts due on invoices

- input a reference if required – for example you might type 'cheque', 'BACS' or 'FP' or a numerical reference relating to the payment

- input the amount of the payment in the 'Amount' box

- click on the 'Receipt' box of the invoice that is being paid

- click on the 'Pay in Full' button at the top (or press F3)

- if cash/settlement discount has been deducted from the payment, enter the actual amount received in the Receipt box and the discount taken in the 'Discount' box

- if there is more than one invoice being paid click on the items being paid as appropriate; the 'Analysis Total' box at the bottom will show a running total of the money allocated

- if there is a long list of invoices and a payment to cover them, click on 'Automatic' at the top and the computer will allocate the payment down the invoice list until it runs out

- if a credit note (type 'SC') has been taken account of in the net payment, this should be dealt with first – see the next section for a full explanation

- check that what you have done is correct and SAVE; details to check are:
  - customer, amount, invoices being paid and amount received

    the amounts in the 'Amount' box and the 'Analysis Total' box should be the same (but see next point)

- if the amount received by way of payment is greater than the amount allocated to outstanding invoices the extra payment will show as a 'Payment on Account' after you have saved – see page 103

- if the amount received by way of payment is less than the amount of the invoice(s) it is settling, the amount received will be allocated as far as possible to the appropriate invoice(s) and the unpaid amount will show as outstanding on the Customer's account – see page 101

- you should print out a Day Books: Customer Receipts (Summary) for these transactions from REPORTS in BANK ACCOUNTS to check that the total of the payments received equals the total input

DEALING WITH CREDIT NOTES

When inputting payments from customers and to suppliers, you may encounter the situation where the amount received (or paid out) is not the same as the amount of the invoice being settled.

For example, if a customer is issued with an invoice for £1,000 and then issued with a credit note for £100 because some of the goods are faulty, the customer will only owe – and pay – £900. The computer screen, however, will show this £900 as two separate lines: an invoice for £1,000 and a credit note for £100. If the £900 cheque received is allocated only against the £1,000, the computer will think a balance of £100 still needs to be paid against this invoice, even though the account balance is nil.

the solution

The credit note needs to be allocated to the balance of the invoice. This is done by:

- clicking on the 'Receipt' box on the credit note line
- clicking on 'Pay in Full' so that the analysis total shows a minus amount
- clicking on the Receipt box on the invoice line and then 'Pay in Full' so that the analysis box shows the payment amount

This procedure can be carried out during or after the payments received routine. In the example below a credit note for £240 is being set off against an invoice for £2,880, the amount received being £2,640.

Note that the procedure for allocating supplier credit notes to supplier invoices works on exactly the same principle.

No.	Type	A/C	Date	Ref	Ex.Ref	Department	Details	T/C	Amount £	Disputed?	Receipt £	Discount £
25	SI	VH001	04/07/2016	10023		n/a	Garden fur...	n/a	2880.00		2880.00	0.00
28	SC	VH001	05/07/2016	551		n/a	Garden fur...	n/a	240.00		240.00	0.00
32	SI	VH001	14/07/2016	10028		n/a	Kennels	n/a	1366.32		0.00	0.00

Analysis Total 2640.00

DEALING WITH UNDERPAYMENTS AND OVERPAYMENTS

Sometimes a customer will send an amount which does not tally with the amount that appears on the customer's statement and the amount on the computer records. For example:

- the customer sends a part payment of an account because he or she is short of money, or thinks a credit note is due
- the customer sends too much money, ignoring a credit note that has been issued or paying the account twice

underpayment

If a customer underpays an account, the amount received is allocated against the relevant invoice. The amount that is still owing will show on the computer records. Here £5,000 has been paid by Cornwood Stud and allocated as part-payment of the opening balance.

The screenshot on the next page shows the activity of Cornwood Stud's account after the part-payment. Note that £726.88 of the opening balance is still outstanding and that a small 'p' is shown to indicate that the invoice has been part paid.

overpayment

If a customer overpays an account, ie pays more than the amount due, there are two ways of dealing with it:

1 The amount can be allocated against any outstanding invoices and the excess shown as a "payment on account"

2 The whole amount can be treated as a "payment on account" and allocated at a later date

In the example at the top of the next page Oliver Cole has paid £1,500. This has been allocated to the outstanding transactions and the excess shown as a payment on account.

The activity on Oliver Cole's account shows the £358.08 overpayment awaiting allocation against future transactions.

RECORDING PAYMENTS TO SUPPLIERS

what documents are involved?

A business often pays its suppliers after it receives a **statement** setting out the amounts due from invoices and any deductions made following the issue of credit notes. This is not a hard and fast rule, however, and it is quite in order to pay individual invoices as and when they are due.

Payment may still be made by cheque, although payments are more likely to be processed electronically by BACS transfer between the banks' computers.

The business will send a **remittance advice** (see page 97) to the supplier giving details of the payment.

supplier payments and the accounting system

Payment to a supplier settling one or more invoices (less any credit notes) needs to be recorded in the accounting system. The entry will:

■ decrease the balance in the bank account (a credit in double-entry)

■ increase the balance in the supplier's account (and the Creditors Control Account) because the supplier will be owed less (a debit in double-entry accounting)

In computer accounting the payment is input once and the two entries will be automatically made from the same screen.

processing the payments

As with customer receipts, the business will normally input a number of payments at one time on a regular basis, for example just after the payment instructions have been prepared.

The payments are input in the SUPPLIER PAYMENT option of PAYMENTS in the BANK ACCOUNTS screen – after the appropriate bank account has been selected.

The procedure for recording the supplier payment is to:

■ input the supplier reference in the box next to the word 'Payee' – this will bring up on-screen the account name and all the outstanding amounts due on invoices

■ input the payment reference under Cheque No and alter the date if the payment date is different

■ input the amount of the payment in the value box

- click on the 'Payment' box of the invoice that is being paid – and click on the 'Pay in full' icon at the top; if there is more than one invoice being paid click on the items being paid as appropriate
- check that what you have done is correct (ie supplier, amount, invoices being paid) and SAVE (refer to page 106 if you wish to print out a remittance advice)
- print out a Day Books: Supplier Payments (Summary) from REPORTS in BANK to check that the total payments issued equals the total input on the computer

Note that when processing supplier payments you may, as with customer payments, have to adjust for credit notes, overpayments and underpayments. These are covered in detail on pages 99-103.

A supplier payment screen is shown below.

No.	Type	A/C	Date	Ref	Ex.Ref	Department	Details	T/C	Amount £	Disputed?	Payment £	Discount £
5	PI	ET001	23/06/2016	16-2808		n/a	Opening B...	n/a	4506.00		4506.00	0.00
34	PI	ET001	05/07/2016	16-2941		n/a	Posts and ...	n/a	1859.16		0.00	0.00

Supplier Payment - Bank Current Account

Clear form / Pay in full (F3) / Wizard / Automatic / Department / Print list / Send to Excel

Bank A/C Ref 1200 — Bank Current Account — Date* 22/07/2016 — Cheque No. Faster paymen

Payee* ET001 — Estate Timber Ltd

Four thousand, five hundred six pounds — £ 4506.00

Tapper Timber

Show All — From / / — To / /

Supplier Balance 1859.16 — Bank Balance 20537.04 — Analysis Total 4506.00

Save — Close

printing remittance advices and cheques

Remittance advices and cheques may be printed once a payment has been processed in Sage.

To print a remittance advice, click on REMITTANCES in the PAYMENTS drop down options in BANK ACCOUNTS. Select the transaction or transactions for which the remittance advice is required, click PRINT and then choose one of the remittance options and click RUN.

To print cheques (with remittance advice attached), click on CHEQUES on the BANK ACCOUNTS toolbar. Pre-printed cheques must be specially ordered.

A printed remittance advice is shown below.

Tapper Timber
Unit 3
Greenslade Way
Stourcastle
ST4 6TG

Tel : 01877 453611
Email : info@tappertimber.co.uk
VAT Reg No. 404 7106 52

REMITTANCE ADVICE

Date	22/07/2016
Account Ref	ET001
Cheque No	Faster paymen

Estate Timber Ltd
Woodbury Farm

Martleford

ST6 5FG

NOTE: All values are shown in Pound Sterling

Date	Ref	Details	Debit	Credit
23/06/2016	16-2808	Opening Balance		4,506.00

Amount Paid	
£	4,506.00

TAPPER TIMBER: PROCESSING PAYMENTS FROM CUSTOMERS AND TO SUPPLIERS

During the month Ross has received some payments from his customers in settlement of their accounts. He has also settled supplier accounts due.

receipts from customers

Payments received from customers are shown below. 'FP rec' stands for Faster Payments receipt. Cheques are paid into the bank on the day of receipt.

Date	Customer		Value	Details
8 July 2016	Oliver Cole & Sons	FP rec	2,904.20	Payment of opening balance
15 July 2016	Victoria Hotel	Cheque	9,900.78	Payment of opening balance
22 July 2016	Cornwood Stud	FP rec	5,000.00	Part-payment of opening bal

These payments are entered into the computer accounting system under CUSTOMER RECEIPT in the BANK ACCOUNTS section as shown on the screen below. This illustrates the Oliver Cole payment being made.

Two further payments have been received as shown below.

Date	Customer		Value	Details
31 July 2016	Oliver Cole & Sons	FP rec	1,500.00	Allocate to all outstanding items and post excess as payment on account.
31 July 2016	Victoria Hotel	Cheque	2,640.00	Payment of invoice 10023 less credit note 551.

Ross allocates the Oliver Cole payment to all outstanding items and posts the excess as payment on account.

© 2016 Sage (UK) Limited. All rights reserved.

Ross prints out a Day Books: Customer Receipts (Detailed) report which shows all the customer payment transactions he has processed and how they have been allocated. He enters a date range of 8 to 31 July. This is shown on the next page.

| Date: | | | | | **Tapper Timber** | | | | | | | **Page:** 1 | |
| Time: | | | | | **Day Books: Customer Receipts (Detailed)** | | | | | | | | |

| **Date From:** | 08/07/2016 | | | | | | | **Bank From:** | | 1200 | | | |
| **Date To:** | 31/07/2016 | | | | | | | **Bank To:** | | 1200 | | | |

| **Transaction From:** | 1 | | | | | | **Customer From:** | | | | |
| **Transaction To:** | 99,999,999 | | | | | | **Customer To:** | | ZZZZZZZZ | | |

Bank: 1200   **Currency:** Pound Sterling

No	Type	A/C	Date	Ref	Details	Net £	Tax £	T/C	Gross £	V	B	Bank Rec. Date
40	SR	OC001	08/07/2016	FP receipt	Sales Receipt	2,904.20	0.00	T9	2,904.20	-	N	
		-	08/07/2016	10013	2904.20 to SI 1							
41	SR	VH001	15/07/2016	Cheque	Sales Receipt	9,900.78	0.00	T9	9,900.78	-	N	
		-	15/07/2016	10016	9900.78 to SI 2							
42	SR	CS001	22/07/2016	FP receipt	Sales Receipt	5,000.00	0.00	T9	5,000.00	-	N	
		-	22/07/2016	10019	5000.00 to SI 3							
46	SR	OC001	31/07/2016	FP receipt	Sales Receipt	1,141.92	0.00	T9	1,141.92	-	N	
		-	31/07/2016	10024	631.92 to SI 26							
		-	31/07/2016	10027	510.00 to SI 31							
47	SA	OC001	31/07/2016	FP receipt	Payment on Account	358.08	0.00	T9	358.08	-	N	
48	SR	VH001	31/07/2016	Cheque	Sales Receipt	2,640.00	0.00	T9	2,640.00	-	N	
		-	31/07/2016	10023	2640.00 to SI 25							
					Totals £	21,944.98	0.00		21,944.98			

payments to suppliers

Ross has checked his supplier invoices against the relevant purchase orders. He has also noted that two suppliers have issued credit notes relating to June invoices. These can be deducted from the amounts due.

The list of payments made directly from the business bank account using Faster Payments is shown below:

Date	Customer	Value	Details
18 July 2016	Chapman Panels	5,972.52	Payment of opening balance less credit note C93
22 July 2016	Estate Timber	4,506.00	Payment of opening balance
26 July 2016	Johnsons Fixings	4,843.62	Payment of opening balance less credit note R281

These payments are entered into the computer accounting system under PAYMENTS/SUPPLIER PAYMENT in the BANK ACCOUNTS section as shown on the screen on the next page. This illustrates the payment to Estate Timber being made.

Ross prints out a remittance advice for each payment (not shown here).

Ross prints out a Day Books: Supplier Payments (Detailed) report which shows all the supplier payment transactions he has processed and how they have been allocated. He enters a date range of 18 to 26 July. This is shown below.

Tapper Timber

Day Books: Supplier Payments (Detailed)

| Date: | | | | | | | | Page: 1 |
| Time: | | | | | | | | |

| Date From: | 18/07/2016 | Bank From: | 1200 |
| DateTo: | 26/07/2016 | Bank To: | 1200 |

| Transaction From: | 1 | Supplier From: | |
| Transaction To: | 99,999,999 | Supplier To: | ZZZZZZZZ |

Bank 1200   **Currency** Pound Sterling

No	Type	A/C	Date	Ref	Details	Net £	Tax £	T/C	Gross £	V	B	Bank Rec Date
43	PP	CP001	18/07/2016	Faster	Purchase Payment	5,972.52	0.00	T9	5,972.52	-	N	
			- 18/07/2016	7611	5972.52 to PI 4							
44	PP	ET001	22/07/2016	Faster	Purchase Payment	4,506.00	0.00	T9	4,506.00	-	N	
			- 22/07/2016	16-2408	4506.00 to PI 5							
45	PP	JF001	26/07/2016	Faster	Purchase Payment	4,843.62	0.00	T9	4,843.62	-	N	
			- 26/07/2016	M41997	4843.62 to PI 6							
					Totals £	15,322.14	0.00		15,322.14			

Chapter Summary

- The bank account is central to the operation of any business as so many transactions pass through it.

- A business can set up not only the bank current account in the computer accounting system, but also a number of other 'money' accounts. These, which include petty cash account and credit card accounts, enable the business to keep track of the processing of money in a variety of forms.

- Payments received from customers who have bought on credit can be processed through the computer accounting system. The accounting system is adjusted in each case by an increase in the bank current account and a reduction of the customer's account balance in the Sales Ledger.

- Payments to suppliers from whom the business has bought on credit can also be processed on the computer and remittance advices printed if required. The accounting entries in this case are a decrease in the bank current account and a reduction in the supplier's account balance in the Purchases Ledger.

- The payment amount in each case (customer or supplier) will usually relate to invoices and credit notes issued. Any overpayment or underpayment can also be recorded.

- It is essential to check the input of payments from customers and to suppliers by printing a report such as a Day Book Report.

Key Terms

current account	the 'everyday' bank account which handles routine receipts and payments
cash payments	payments made straightaway
credit payments	payments made at a later date following the issue of an invoice to a customer or by a supplier
remittance advice	a document that tells a business that a payment is being made
payments on account	an overpayment or amount that is not allocated to specific transactions

Activities

7.1 What do the icons Bank payment, Supplier payment, Bank receipt and Customer receipt represent within the Bank accounts module?

7.2 Why is it helpful if a business receives a remittance advice when payment is made direct to its bank account from a customer settling an invoice or account?

7.3 What entries to the accounting system will be made when a business receives a payment from a credit customer and makes a payment to a supplier?

7.4 What printout from a computer accounting system lists payments made to suppliers in any particular date range?

TAPPER TIMBER INPUTTING TASKS

Set the program date as 31 July 2016.

Task 1

Enter the following customer payments in BANK ACCOUNTS/CUSTOMER RECEIPT.

Date	Customer		Value	Details
8 July 2016	Oliver Cole & Sons	FP rec	2,904.20	Payment of opening balance
15 July 2016	Victoria Hotel	Cheque	9,900.78	Payment of opening balance
22 July 2016	Cornwood Stud	FP rec	5,000.00	Part-payment of opening balance

Task 2

Enter the following Faster payments made to suppliers in BANK ACCOUNTS/PAYMENTS/SUPPLIER PAYMENT. Print out a remittance advice for the payment to Chapman Panels.

Date	Customer	Value	Details
18 July 2016	Chapman Panels	5,972.52	Payment of opening balance less credit note C93
22 July 2016	Estate Timber	4,506.00	Payment of opening balance
26 July 2016	Johnsons Fixings	4,843.62	Payment of opening balance less credit note R281

Task 3

Enter two further customer payments:

Date	Customer		Value	Details
31 July 2016	Oliver Cole & Sons	FP rec	1,500.00	Allocate to all outstanding items and post excess as payment on account.
31 July 2016	Victoria Hotel	Cheque	2,640.00	Payment of invoice 10023 less credit note 551

Task 4

Print the following reports and check them against those on pages 187 and 188:

(a)   Detailed Day Books for all customer receipts in the date range 8 to 31 July.

(b)   Detailed Day Books for all supplier payments in the date range 18 to 26 July.

(c)   Trial Balance as at 31 July 2016.

Reminder! Have you made a back-up?

8 Cash receipts and payments

this chapter covers...

■ The previous chapter explained how payments settling invoices are recorded in a computer accounting system. These payments received from customers and made to suppliers settle up 'credit sales' where invoices are issued when the sale is made and payment is made later.

■ A business will also process a substantial number of varied 'cash payments' where the money is transferred at the same time as the transaction. Note that 'cash' does not just mean notes and coins in this context; it means immediate payment.

Examples of these payments (and receipts) include:

– money received from sales – over the counter sales or online sales

– money spent on purchases – buying stock and materials for use in the business

– running expenses paid – wages, power bills, rent

– items bought for permanent use in the business – fixed assets not bought on credit

– loans made to the business

– money (capital) put into the business by the owner(s)

■ A computer accounting system will record these 'cash' items in a different way from the 'credit' items seen in the previous chapter.

■ The transactions mentioned so far involve payments which are made straight through the bank current account. A business may also use other funds for making payments and receiving money. These are covered in the next chapter.

THE BANK ACCOUNTS

The previous chapter started by looking at how different bank accounts can be set up in a computerised accounting system. Whereas the last chapter concentrated on the use of the Bank Current Account for making payments for credit transactions, this chapter examines the way in which cash payments (immediate payments) are recorded.

The BANK screen shown below (the default accounts screen) explains the icons that you will be using in this chapter.

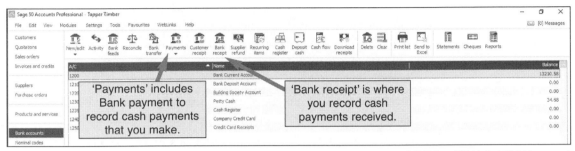

CASH RECEIPTS

Cash sales made by a business are usually sales made at a checkout or through an online shop. 'Cash' here means 'immediate payment'.

Receipts from cash sales can be made by cash, cheque, debit or credit card and BACS. The business should ensure the money is paid into the bank current account as soon as possible, so that it can be used to meet payments the business may have made or may have to make.

The input screen for cash sales is reached from the BANK RECEIPT icon on the BANK ACCOUNTS toolbar. It looks like this:

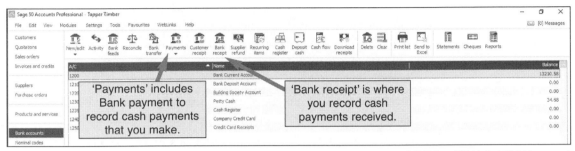

inputting bank receipts

Cash sales paid straight into the bank may be input from the bank paying-in slips recorded in the business cash book or from a sales listing sheet. These receipts are input as follows:

- select the computer bank account number

- enter the date (usually the date the money is paid into the bank)

- enter a reference (this can be the reference number of the paying-in slip)

- input the appropriate nominal code (N/C) for the type of sales involved

- enter a description of the payment (eg 'Fencing sales') under 'Details'

- enter the net amount of the sales (ie the sales amount excluding VAT) and then click on T1 if the goods are standard rated for VAT – the computer will then automatically calculate the VAT amount for you and show it in the right-hand column

- check that the VAT amount shown agrees with your figure and change it on-screen if it does not – there may be a rounding difference

- check the input details and totals and then SAVE

VAT posting

The rates of VAT (**tax codes**) that you are most likely to come across are:

T1	standard rate (20% at the time of writing)
T2	exempt from VAT – eg postage stamps, insurance
T0	zero-rated, ie VAT could be charged but it is zero at the moment – eg books, food and some children's clothes
T9	transactions not involving VAT

If you only have a VAT-inclusive figure and do not know what the VAT amount is, enter the total figure in the 'Net' column and click on 'Calc.Net' at the top of the screen, or press F9. The computer then automatically calculates and shows the Net amount and the VAT.

See images at the top of the next page.

The VAT values entered in a computerised accounting program are posted to separate VAT accounts. One account records Sales VAT (called output tax by HMRC) and another records Purchase VAT (input tax). The difference between the balances of these two accounts is the amount due to HMRC.

Click Calculate net (or F9) to separate Net and VAT

Enter total (VAT inclusive) figure

Net and VAT figures are automatically calculated

other cash receipts

You can also enter other cash (= not credit) receipts using the same Bank Receipts screen. Examples include:

- money invested by the owner(s) of the business – capital (N/C 3000)
- loans and grants from outside bodies (N/C 2300)
- income from other sources such as rent received (N/C 4904), bank interest or commission received (N/C 4902)

This money is likely to be received in the form of a cheque or bank transfer.

CASH PAYMENTS

Most credit payments made by businesses, as we saw in the previous chapter, are to suppliers for goods and services provided and paid for on invoice. But businesses also have to make payments on a day-to-day cash basis (immediate payment) for running costs and expenses such as wages, telephone bills, owner drawings and sundry (miscellaneous) expenses. Cash payments may also be made to suppliers where no credit terms have been agreed.

These payments are input from BANK PAYMENT reached by clicking on the PAYMENTS drop down menu on the BANK ACCOUNTS toolbar. See the example shown below.

| 🏛 Bank Payments | | | | | | | | | | | — □ ✕ |

| Clear form | Print Cheque | Insert row (F7) | Remove row (F8) | Copy cell above (F6) | Copy cell above +1 (Shift + F6) | Calculate net (F9) | Memorise | Recall | Print list | Send to Excel |

| Bank | Bank Current Account | | | Tax Rate | 0.00 |
| N/C | Drawings | | | Total | 4915.52 |

Bank*	Date*	Ref	Ex.Ref	N/C*	Departmen	Project Ref	Cost Code	Details	Net	T/C*	Tax
1200	01/07/2016	122992		5000	0			Materials pu...	1529.60	T1	305.92
1200	07/07/2016	Debit card		6201	0			Advertising	900.00	T1	180.00
1200	08/07/2016	Faster p...		3050	0		✓	Drawings	2000.00	T9	0.00

| | 4429.60 | | 485.92 |

| | Save | Close |

inputting cash payments

Cash payments can be input from the handwritten business **cash book** (if one is used), or from the bills being paid (which should show any VAT element). The procedure for inputting is:

- select the computer bank account number

- enter the date (the date the payment is made)

- enter a reference (if there is one)

- input the appropriate nominal code (N/C) for the type of payment involved

- enter a brief description of the nature of the payment (eg 'Telephone') under 'Details'

■ enter the net amount of the payment (ie the amount excluding VAT) and then click on T1 if the product is standard rated for VAT – the computer will then automatically calculate the VAT amount for you and show it in the right-hand column

■ check that the VAT amount shown agrees with your figure and change it on-screen if it does not – there may be a rounding difference

a note on VAT

The VAT rates used here are:

T1	the purchases and advertising are standard rated
T9	drawings do not involve VAT

The code for a zero-rated item would have been T0. The code for a VAT exempt item would have been T2.

checking the input data

It is important to check your input for each item against the source data for the input. You will see that the screen on the previous page has running total boxes below the Net and Tax columns. There is also a Total (Net plus Tax) box at the top. These boxes will all update as you enter the transactions.

If you are entering the data for a number of transactions you should add up the three 'batch' totals (Net, VAT and Total) and check them against the screen figures in the total boxes when you have finished your data entry.

As a final check you should print out a Day Book report (see extract below) from Reports in BANK ACCOUNTS and check the entries against your handwritten records.

Date: Time:					**Tapper Timber** **Day Books: Bank Payments (Detailed)**						Page:	1	
Date From: **Date To:**	01/07/2016 08/07/2016									**Bank From:** **Bank To:**	1200 1200		
Transaction From: **Transaction To:**	1 99,999,999									**N/C From:** **N/C To:**	99999999		
Dept From: **Dept To:**	0 999												

| Bank: | 1200 | | **Currency:** | Pound Sterling | | | | | | | | **Bank Rec.** | |
No	**Type**	**N/C**	**Date**	**Ref**	**Details**	**Dept**	**Net £**	**Tax £**	**T/C**	**Gross £**	**V**	**B**	**Date**
51	BP	5000	01/07/2016	122992	Materials	0	1,529.60	305.92	T1	1,835.52	N	N	
52	BP	6201	07/07/2016	Debit card	Advertising	0	900.00	180.00	T1	1,080.00	N	N	
53	BP	3050	08/07/2016	Faster	Drawings	0	2,000.00	0.00	T9	2,000.00	-	N	
						Totals £	4,429.60	485.92		4,915.52			

**Case
Study**

TAPPER TIMBER:
CASH RECEIPTS AND PAYMENTS

Ross has to input the various cash receipts and payments received and made during the month.

cash receipts

Tapper Timber paid takings of cash into the bank current account several times during July. The first amount, paid in on 4 July, is shown below. The reference quoted is the paying-in slip reference.

Date	Details	Net amount £	VAT £	Total £	Reference
4/07/16	Garden furniture cash sales	4,680.55	936.11	5,616.66	10736
4/07/16	Animal housing cash sales	3,251.00	650.20	3,901.20	10737
Totals		7,931.55	1,586.31	9,517.86	

These sales receipts are entered into the computer accounting system on the BANK RECEIPTS screen of the BANK ACCOUNTS toolbar. Note that the Bank Current Account and the appropriate nominal sales codes (N/C) are used each time.

Ross can use some helpful features when inputting. When in a line and wanting to copy the box above (eg the bank account number or the date), he presses F6; when wanting to raise the number in the box by one (eg reference number), he presses Shift F6.

Bank*	Date*	Ref	Ex.Ref	N/C*	Department	Project Ref	Details	Net	T/C*	Tax
1200	04/07/2016	10736		4001	0		Garden furnit...	4680.55	T1	936.11
1200	04/07/2016	10737		4003	0		Animal housin...	3251.00	T1	650.20

Bank: Bank Current Account; N/C: Animal housing; Tax Rate 20.00; Total 9517.86; 7931.55; 1586.31

Ross then checks his listing totals against the on-screen totals for accuracy and hits SAVE. He prints out a Day Books: Bank Receipts (Detailed) report for 4 July as shown below.

Date: **Tapper Timber**   **Page:** 1
Time: **Day Books: Bank Receipts (Detailed)**

Date From: 04/07/2016		**Bank From:** 1200
Date To: 04/07/2016		**Bank To:** 1200
Transaction From: 1		**N/C From:**
Transaction To: 99,999,999		**N/C To:** 99999999
Dept From: 0		
Dept To: 999		

Bank: 1200   **Currency:** Pound Sterling

No	Type	N/C	Date	Ref	Details	Dept	Net £	Tax £	T/C	Gross £	V	B	Bank Rec. Date
49	BR	4001	04/07/2016	10736	Garden furniture	0	4,680.55	936.11	T1	5,616.66	N	N	
50	BR	4003	04/07/2016	10737	Animal housing	0	3,251.00	650.20	T1	3,901.20	N	N	
						Totals £	7,931.55	1,586.31		9,517.86			

cash payments

Tapper Timber made a number of cash payments for normal day-to-day running expenses during July. Some are shown below.

Date	Details	Net amount £	VAT £	Total £	Reference
1/07/16	Materials purchased	1,529.60	305.92	1,835.52	Cheque 122992
7/07/16	Advertising	900.00	180.00	1,080.00	Debit card
8/07/16	Drawings	2,000.00	No VAT	2,000.00	Faster payments
Totals		4,429.60	485.92	4,915.52	

These payments are entered into the computer accounting system in the BANK PAYMENTS option on the BANK ACCOUNTS toolbar. Note that the Bank Current Account and the appropriate nominal code (N/C) are used each time.

If Ross needs to insert or delete lines when entering data, he can press F7 to insert a blank line between two lines already entered, or F8 to delete a line already entered.

Ross then checks his listing totals against the on-screen totals for accuracy and hits SAVE. He prints out a Day Books: Bank Payments (Detailed) report as shown below.

Date: **Tapper Timber**   **Page:** 1
Time: **Day Books: Bank Payments (Detailed)**

Date From:	01/07/2016			**Bank From:**	1200
Date To:	08/07/2016			**Bank To:**	1200
Transaction From:	1			**N/C From:**	
Transaction To:	99,999,999			**N/C To:**	99999999
Dept From:	0				
Dept To:	999				

Bank: 1200   **Currency:** Pound Sterling

No	Type	N/C	Date	Ref	Details	Dept	Net £	Tax £	T/C	Gross £	V	B	Bank Rec. Date
51	BP	5000	01/07/2016	122992	Materials	0	1,529.60	305.92	T1	1,835.52	N	N	
52	BP	6201	07/07/2016	Debit card	Advertising	0	900.00	180.00	T1	1,080.00	N	N	
53	BP	3050	08/07/2016	Faster	Drawings	0	2,000.00	0.00	T9	2,000.00	-	N	
					Totals £		4,429.60	485.92		4,915.52			

CASH RECEIPTS AND PAYMENTS AND THE ACCOUNTING SYSTEM

It is important to appreciate how the cash receipts and payments in this chapter relate to the accounting system of a business, particularly if you are also studying double-entry bookkeeping.

Remember that transactions involve debits and credits and that the debit amount always equals the credit amount. Because of the VAT included in many sales and purchases, these transactions may involve three entries:

- the amount posted to the bank account (the full amount)
- the 'net' amount (the amount before VAT is added on) posted to the sales account or purchases (or expense) account
- any VAT involved in the transaction being posted to Sales or Purchases VAT account

The whole cash payment system is summarised in the linked diagram opposite. This shows how the money comes into and out of the bank account and illustrates how the double-entry bookkeeping works. If you are not studying double-entry, just concentrate on the types of receipts and payments and study how they are input.

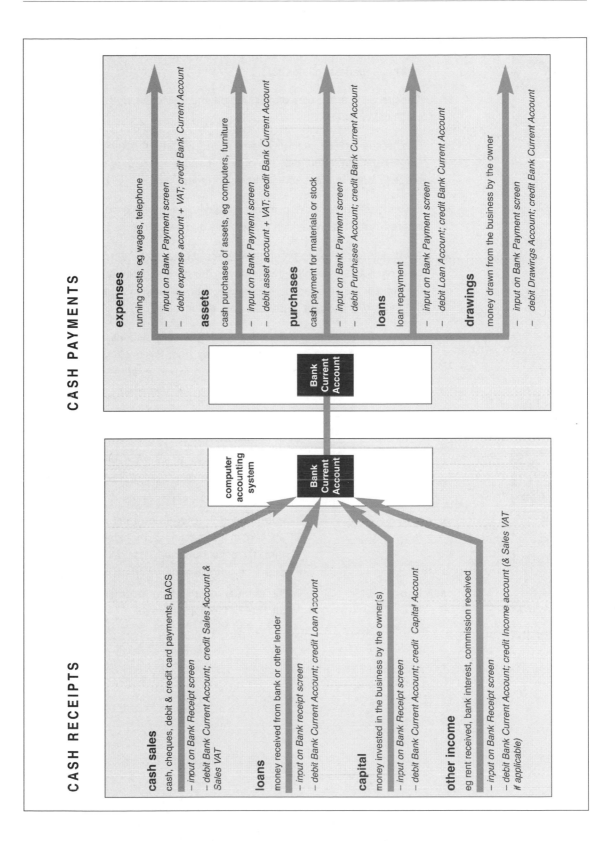

Chapter Summary

■ Cash payments are payments which are immediate, unlike credit payments which are made at a later date.

■ Cash receipts and payments include payment by cash, cheques, debit and credit cards and BACS.

■ Businesses receive cash payments from a variety of sources: cash sales, loans, capital introduced by the owner(s) and other income such as rent of property, bank interest and commission received.

■ Businesses make cash payments for day-to-day running costs, purchases where no credit is given, loan repayments and owner drawings.

■ A computer accounting program will record cash payments coming in – ie cash receipts – by adding the money to the bank account and by adjusting the appropriate other account (eg sales, loan, capital, income account) and the Sales VAT account (if there is any VAT involved).

■ A computer accounting program will record cash payments going out – ie cash payments – by deducting the money from the bank account and by adjusting the appropriate other account (eg expense, asset purchase) and the Purchases VAT account (if there is any VAT involved).

Key Terms

cash sales — sales made where payment is immediate

current account — the 'everyday' bank account which handles routine receipts and payments

tax codes — a term used to refer to the rate of VAT which is applied to transactions; T1 refers to standard rate, T0 to the zero rate, T2 to VAT exempt items and T9 to transactions which do not involve VAT

cash book — the manual record which records money paid in and out of the bank account

Activities

8.1   From which icon on the BANK ACCOUNTS toolbar will the screen needed for recording a cash sale from a customer be reached? BANK RECEIPT or CUSTOMER RECEIPT?

8.2   From which icon on the BANK ACCOUNTS toolbar will the screen needed for recording a cash purchase from a supplier be reached? BANK PAYMENT or SUPPLIER PAYMENT?

8.3   Complete the sentences below using the following computer account names:

• Bank   • Purchases   • Sales   • Purchases VAT   • Sales VAT

(a)   A business makes a cash sale for £120.00, which is made up of £100 net and £20.00 VAT. The postings to the computer accounts will be:

£120.00 to .... account

£100.00 to .... account

£20.00 to .... account

(b)   A business makes a cash purchase for £960, which is made up of £800 net and £160 VAT. The postings to the computer accounts will be:

£160.00 to .... account

£960.00 to .... account

£800.00 to .... account

8.4   Businesses from time-to-time pay into the bank cash payments which are not received from cash sales. Give three examples of this type of cash receipt.

TAPPER TIMBER INPUTTING TASKS

Set the program date as 31 July 2016.

Task 1

Enter the following bank receipts. Check your totals before saving and print out a Day Books: Bank Receipts (Detailed) report covering the entire date range of transactions. Check it against the report on page 188.

Date	Details	Net amount £	VAT £	Total £	Reference
4/07/16	Garden furniture cash sales	4,680.55	936.11	5,616.66	10736
4/07/16	Animal housing cash sales	3,251.00	650.20	3,901.20	10737
11/07/16	Fencing cash sales	865.70	173.14	1,038.84	10738
11/07/16	Sheds cash sales	5,660.50	1,132.10	6,792.60	10739
Totals		14,457.75	2,891.55	17,349.30	

Task 2

Enter the following bank payments. Check your totals before saving and print out a Day Books: Bank Payments (Detailed) report covering the entire date range of transactions. Check it against the report on page 189.

Date	Details	Net amount £	VAT £	Total £	Reference
1/07/16	Materials purchased	1,529.60	305.92	1,835.52	Cheque 122992
7/07/16	Advertising	900.00	180.00	1,080.00	Debit card
8/07/16	Drawings	2,000.00	No VAT	2,000.00	Faster payments
13/07/16	Telephone bill	312.00	62.40	374.40	Faster payments
18/07/16	Equipment hire	456.00	91.20	547.20	Debit card
Totals		5,197.60	639.52	5,837.12	

Task 3

(a) On 27 July Ross writes a personal cheque for additional owner capital to be paid into the business. The amount is £5,000.00. VAT is not applicable.

(b) On 29 July he writes a business cheque (number 122993) for £21,594.00 (£17,995.00 plus VAT £3,599.00) for a new delivery vehicle for use within the business.

Enter these two transactions using the dates given. The relevant nominal codes are Capital and Motor Vehicles.

Task 4

Print out a trial balance as at 31 July to check the accuracy of your input to date. Check yours against the trial balance on page 189. Note particularly the increases in Capital and Motor Vehicle accounts.

9 Bank accounts, petty cash and recurring entries

this chapter covers...

■ *The previous chapter explained how cash payments made directly in and out of the bank current account are recorded in a computer accounting system. 'Cash payment' here means 'immediate payment'. It can involve cash, cheques, payments by debit and credit card and BACS.*

■ *The computer program also enables a business to use or set up accounts to record other funds of money held by the business. These funds are classified as 'Bank' accounts, but the money is not necessarily held at a bank – it may be held within the business.*

■ *One example is the petty cash account – a cash fund held under lock and key in the office, used for making small purchases and payments. The money for this account will come from the bank current account and be recorded by a Bank Transfer.*

■ *If a business – a shop for example – receives cash payments and then holds them on the premises for a length of time before paying them into the bank, it may decide to use a Cash Register account to record the takings.*

When the money is eventually paid into the bank, the business will record a Bank Transfer from Cash Register to show the money being paid into the bank.

■ *Businesses may need to record regular payments made in and out of the bank current account. Examples include standing orders and direct debits for outgoing payments of insurance premiums and business rates and incoming receipts of rent from tenants.*

The Recurring Items facility enables the business to set up the payments so that they are recorded automatically in the accounts with one click.

THE BANK ACCOUNTS IN COMPUTER ACCOUNTING

The bank accounts and all the functions associated with them are found in Sage by clicking on BANK ACCOUNTS in the vertical toolbar.

The accounts listed come from the default list in the Chart of Accounts. The business does not have to adopt all the accounts, but may use some of them if it needs them. It can also set up new accounts within the appropriate account number range by clicking NEW/EDIT on the toolbar. A summary of the Sage bank accounts is on page 95.

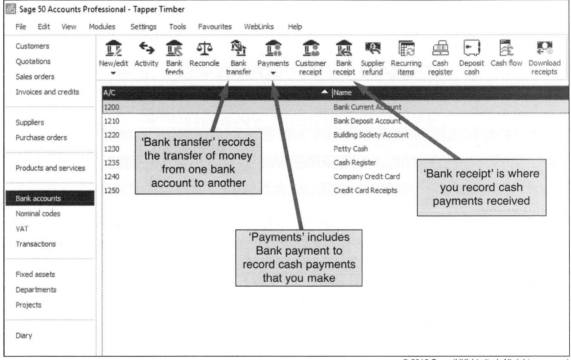

when is a bank account not a bank account?

The first three types of account shown on the above screen are actually maintained at the bank or building society. They are true 'bank' accounts. The petty cash and cash register accounts are not kept at the bank but within the business. They are used to record money funds within the business which originally came from the bank or will be paid into the bank. The two credit card accounts are used to record outgoing and incoming card transactions.

transfers between accounts

A BANK TRANSFER facility on the BANK ACCOUNTS toolbar records movements between the 'bank' accounts. The screen below shows a transfer of £5,000 from the current account (1200) to the deposit account (1210).

OPENING UP A PETTY CASH ACCOUNT

what is a petty cash payment?

Petty cash is a float of cash – notes and coins – kept in an office, normally in a locked tin. It provides employees with the cash to make small purchases for the business, eg stationery, postage stamps and business taxi fares. The petty cash float is topped up with cash periodically.

The document used is the petty cash voucher (see below). When a payment is made, a petty cash voucher is completed and the appropriate evidence of payment is attached, for example:

- a till receipt from a shop or a Post Office receipt for stamps
- a rail or bus ticket or a receipt from a taxi firm

The cash can be paid out (or refunded) when the voucher is completed and authorised.

petty cash voucher			Number *507*	
		date	*16 May 2016*	
description			amount	
			£	p
Payment				
Envelopes			6	*00*
		VAT	*1*	20
Receipt obtained			7	20
signature	*T Harris*			
authorised	*R Patel*			

petty cash and the accounting system

Petty cash is a fund of money kept in the business in the same way as the bank current account is a fund of money kept in the bank. A 'bank' account will be set up for petty cash which will record all the transactions:

■ transfers of cash into petty cash from the bank current account

■ payments out of petty cash to pay for small expense items

■ payments into petty cash from small receipts

transfers into petty cash

In Sage the Petty Cash account is classed as a bank account, although, of course, the money is not in the bank.

When cash is needed to top up the petty cash a reimbursement request document may be raised. The business will then draw cash at the bank and then put the money in the cash tin. The computer program requires the business to input the transaction as a BANK TRANSFER from the BANK ACCOUNTS toolbar. In the screen below, the business has drawn £100 at the bank to provide the cash.

From: 1200   Bank Current Account
To: 1230   Petty Cash

From*	To*	Date*	Ref	Ex.Ref	Details	Department	Payment Amount*
1200	1230	01/07/2016	TRANS		From bank to petty cash	0	100.00

payments out of petty cash

Payments out of Petty Cash Account are handled in exactly the same way on the computer as payments out of Bank Current Account, but with the Petty Cash account selected. The PAYMENTS/BANK PAYMENT screen is reached through the BANK ACCOUNTS toolbar. The details are then input from the petty cash vouchers or the petty cash book in which they are recorded.

The screen on the next page shows the input of the petty cash voucher for stationery shown on the opposite page.

Bank Payments

Clear form | Print Cheque | Insert row (F7) | Remove row (F8) | Copy cell above (F6) | Copy cell above +1 (Shift + F6) | Calculate net (F9) | Memorise | Recall | Print list | Send to Excel

Bank: Petty Cash   Tax Rate 20.00
N/C: Office Stationery   Total 7.20

Bank*	Date*	Ref	Ex.Ref	N/C*	Department	Project Ref	Cost Code	Details	Net	T/C*	Tax
1230	16/05/2016	507		7502	0			Envelopes	6.00	T1	1.20

6.00   1.20

Save | Close

receipts into petty cash

There may be occasions when cash is received into the petty cash fund. For example, if staff are allowed to buy stamps or stationery from the business. This is recorded much like a cash sale (see previous chapter/page 115). Select BANK RECEIPT to enter the details of the transaction.

The screen below shows the input of a petty cash receipt for the sale of Stationery. Note that the nominal code used is still the code for Stationery; the sale simply reduces the cost of stationery to the business by the value of stationery sold. VAT is accounted for in the normal way.

Bank Receipts

Clear form | Pay by card | Insert row (F7) | Remove row (F8) | Copy cell above (F6) | Copy cell above +1 (Shift + F6) | Calculate net (F9) | Memorise | Recall | Print list | Send to Excel

Bank: Petty Cash   Tax Rate 20.00
N/C: Office Stationery   Total 6.00

Bank*	Date*	Ref	Ex.Ref	N/C*	Department	Project Ref	Details	Net	T/C*	Tax
1230	18/05/2016	815		7502	0		Sale of statio...	5.00	T1	1.00

5.00   1.00

Save | Close

Points to remember are:

■ the bank account number used is the Petty Cash Account number

■ the reference is the petty cash voucher number

■ petty cash vouchers and their receipts will not always show the VAT amount – the VAT and net amount can be calculated on the computer by inputting the full amount under 'Net' and then clicking on 'Calc.Net' at the top of the screen (using T1 code to denote standard rate VAT)

■ when the details have been checked you should SAVE

■ the details can also be checked against a Cash Payments Day Book printout if required (accessed through REPORTS in BANK ACCOUNTS)

TAPPER TIMBER:
SETTING UP THE PETTY CASH SYSTEM

At the beginning of July Ross Tapper tops up his petty cash system. The situation at the end of the month is as follows:

• Ross notes that he drew cash of £100 at the bank on 1 July.

• The £100 cash was transferred to the petty cash tin on 1 July.

• The tin contains three vouchers for payments made during the month – these are shown below and on the next page. They are ready for entry in the petty cash account as part of the month-end routine.

Voucher PC101 shows the VAT included in the total (standard rate: T1)

Voucher PC102 does not have any VAT in it (postage stamps are exempt: T2)

Voucher PC103 does not show the VAT included in the total (standard rate: T1) because it was not shown on the original receipt

The tin contains one voucher for a receipt – PC104

petty cash voucher		Number *PC101*
	date	*7 July 2016*

description		amount
Payment *Cleaning materials*	£ 36	p 00
	VAT 7	20
Receipt obtained	43	20

signature *Nicky Smith*

authorised *Ross Tapper*

petty cash voucher

Number *PC102*

date   *14 July 2016*

description		amount	
		£	p
Payment *Postage stamps*		25	00
	VAT		
Receipt obtained		25	00

signature   *Nicky Smith*

authorised   *Ross Tapper*

---

petty cash voucher

Number *PC103*

date   *20 July 2016*

description		amount	
		£	p
Payment *Envelopes*			
Receipt obtained (VAT included but not shown separately)	VAT	19	20

signature   *Nicky Smith*

authorised   *Ross Tapper*

---

petty cash voucher

Number *PC104*

date   *25 July 2016*

description		amount	
		£	p
Receipt *A4 paper sold to member of staff*		3	00
	VAT	0	60
		3	60

signature   *Lotte Hunt*

authorised   *Ross Tapper*

the transfer to petty cash

Ross first inputs the £100 transfer from the Bank Current Account to the Petty Cash Account. The screen is illustrated below.

inputting the payments

The petty cash payments are entered into the computer accounting system through PAYMENTS/BANK PAYMENT on the BANK ACCOUNTS toolbar.

The bank Petty Cash Account number and the appropriate nominal code (N/C) are used each time. The nominal codes are taken from the default nominal list.

The reference in each case is the relevant petty cash voucher number.

Postage stamps are VAT-exempt. The VAT on the third petty cash payment voucher was not on the receipt but has been calculated on-screen by inputting the total amount of £19.20 in the 'Net' column and clicking on 'Calc.Net' at the top of the screen:

Ross checks the batch total with the total of the vouchers and when he is happy that all the details are correct he hits SAVE. The Day Book Report will now show the petty cash payments. Note that the transaction code is 'CP' (second column from the left). This stands for 'Cash Payment'. This distinguishes the petty cash payments from payments from the bank current account (input through the same screen). These payments have the code 'BP' which stands for 'Bank Payment'.

Date:	14/01/2016		**Tapper Timber**						Page:	1		
Time:	09:57:25		**Day Books: Cash Payments (Detailed)**									

Date From:	07/07/2016							Bank From:	1230	
Date To:	20/07/2016							Bank To:	1230	
Transaction From:	1							N/C From:		
Transaction To:	99,999,999							N/C To:	99999999	
Dept From:	0									
Dept To:	999									

Bank: 1230   Currency: Pound Sterling

No	Type	N/C	Date	Ref	Details	Dept	Net £	Tax £	T/C	Gross £	V	B	Bank Rec. Date
62	CP	7801	07/07/2016	PC101	Cleaning materials	0	36.00	7.20	T1	43.20	N	-	
63	CP	7501	14/07/2016	PC102	Postage stamps	0	25.00	0.00	T2	25.00	N	-	
64	CP	7502	20/07/2016	PC103	Envelopes	0	16.00	3.20	T1	19.20	N	-	
					Totals £		<u>77.00</u>	<u>10.40</u>		<u>87.40</u>			

inputting the receipt

The Petty Cash receipt is entered into the computer accounting system on the BANK RECEIPTS screen of the BANK ACCOUNTS toolbar.

The bank Petty Cash Account number and the appropriate nominal code (N/C) is used.

VAT has been shown separately on the voucher.

Ross could print out a Day Books: Cash Receipts (Detailed) report if he wished (not shown here).

CARD ACCOUNTS

use of company credit cards

Credit cards are often issued by an employer for use by their employees when they are out on business – for example a sales representative who needs to buy fuel for the company car and to take a client out to lunch. All expenses are billed to the company on the credit card statement and are checked by the management to make sure that the expenses are valid claims.

company credit card payments in the accounts

The business with a computer accounting system can make use of the Credit Card Account in the BANK ACCOUNTS module. This will be used to record all card payments using the BANK PAYMENT screen seen earlier in this chapter, but inputting the payments to the Company Credit Card Account.

When the business pays the credit card bill, the total amount owing to the credit card company will be transferred, using BANK TRANSFER, from the Bank Current Account to the Company Credit Card account.

credit/debit card receipt accounts

A business using computer accounting might also open up an account in BANK ACCOUNTS to record credit and debit card receipts. Totals will then be transferred to the current account. Alternatively, these receipts can be entered directly into the current account. Totals should be reconciled with the advices from the card merchant.

USING A CASH RECEIPTS ACCOUNT

We have seen so far that cash receipts – for example the cash and cheque takings from a shop – are best paid into the bank current account as soon as possible. This reduces the risk of theft and means that the business has the use of the money earlier rather than later.

There may be a case, however, where a business keeps its cash takings on the premises for some time before paying in. This could happen when a week's takings of a shop, for example, are paid in the following Monday. The business here could use the Cash Register Account in BANK ACCOUNTS to record the money fund kept on the premises. The procedure would be:

■ select the Cash Register Account in BANK ACCOUNTS

- enter the totals of daily takings in BANK RECEIPT from the BANK ACCOUNTS menu – the totals could be taken from the various till listings or a summary. Ensure that the VAT element is correctly posted

- using BANK TRANSFER from the BANK ACCOUNTS menu to record the amounts when they are paid into the bank current account – the source document is the paying-in slip and the transfer is made from Cash Register Account to Bank Current Account

The BANK RECEIPT and BANK TRANSFER screens are shown below.

Bank Receipts

Clear form | Pay by card | Insert row (F7) | Remove row (F8) | Copy cell above (F6) | Copy cell above +1 (Shift + F6) | Calculate net (F9) | Memorise | Recall | Print list | Send to Excel

| Bank | Cash Register | | Tax Rate | 20.00 |
| N/C | Sales - Fencing | | Total | 5375.10 |

Bank*	Date*	Ref	Ex.Ref	N/C*	Department	Project Ref	Details	Net	T/C*	Tax
1235	15/07/2016	T001		4002	0		Sheds cash s...	3015.85	T1	603.17
1235	15/07/2016	T002		4000	0		Fencing cash ...	1463.40	T1	292.68
								4479.25		895.85

Save | Close

Here the cash takings for week ending 15 July are recorded in BANK RECEIPTS.

Bank Transfer

Clear form | Insert row (F7) | Remove row (F8) | Copy cell above (F6) | Copy cell above +1 (Shift + F6) | Memorise | Recall | Print list | Send to Excel

From: 1235 Cash Register
To: 1200 Bank Current Account

From*	To*	Date*	Ref	Ex.Ref	Details	Department	Payment Amount*
1235	1200	18/07/2016	10740		From cash register to bank	0	5375.10

Here the takings for the week are being paid into the bank on a paying-in slip on Monday. The amount is transferred from Cash Register Account to Bank Current Account. The balance on the Cash Register Account should then revert to nil as all the money will have left the premises.

RECURRING PAYMENTS AND RECEIPTS

Recurring entries are payments or transfers which are made monthly or weekly or at other intervals. Businesses, for example:

- *receive* recurring payments, for example rent from an office owned
- *make* recurring payments, for example loan repayments, insurance premiums, rent and rates paid

These payments are often made direct from the bank account of the payer to the bank account of the recipient ('beneficiary') by direct debit or standing order.

Payments due are often recorded on a document called a 'Standing order/Direct debit schedule'. If a business operates a manual accounting system these payments will be written individually in the cash book each time they are made or received – a laborious and time-consuming process. A business using a computer accounting system can automate this procedure.

setting up recurring entries in Sage

The RECURRING entries routine is reached from the RECURRING ITEMS icon on the BANK ACCOUNTS toolbar.

The RECURRING ITEMS screen shows any existing entries already set up. If there are none, the screen will be blank.

To add a recurring entry, click 'Add' at the top of the screen.

Now study the Case Study on the next two pages.

Case Study

TAPPER TIMBER: SETTING UP RECURRING ENTRIES

setting up a recurring payment

Tapper Timber pays annual premises insurance on a monthly payment plan, costing £85.00 per month and payable on 15th of each month.

Ross sets this up as a recurring payment using the RECURRING ITEMS icon on the BANK ACCOUNTS toolbar. He clicks the Add button to input the details as shown on the next page.

Add / Edit Recurring Entry   ✕

Recurring Entry From / To

Bank A/C*	1200 ⌄	Bank Current Account
Nominal Code*	7104 ⌄	Premises Insurance

Recurring Entry Details

Transaction Type	Bank/Cash/Credit Card Payment ⌄
Transaction Ref	DD
Transaction Details	Malcaster Insurance - premises insurance
Department*	0 ⌄ Default

Posting Frequency

Every*	1 Month(s) ⌄	Total Required Postings	12
Start Date*	15/07/2016	Finish Date	15/06/2017
Next Posting Date	15/07/2016	Suspend Posting ?	☐
Last Posted			

Posting Amounts

Net Amount	85.00	Tax Code* T2 0.00 ⌄	VAT	0.00

OK   Cancel

Note the following:

- He inputs the bank account (1200) and the nominal code (7104)
- He chooses Bank/Cash/Credit Card Payment
- The Transaction Ref is 'DD' (for Direct Debit)
- The Transaction Details explain what the payment is for
- The posting frequency is once a month
- The start date is 15 July 2016
- The number of Total Required Postings is 12
- The Net Amount and VAT (Tax) Code (T2) are entered

setting up a recurring receipt

Tapper Timber lets part of the secure yard at their business unit to a fellow trader who pays £200 on 20th of each month by standing order. This arrangement is for six months.

Ross sets this up as a recurring receipt using the RECURRING ITEMS icon on the BANK ACCOUNTS toolbar. He clicks the Add button to input the details as shown below.

Add / Edit Recurring Entry   ✕

Recurring Entry From / To

| Bank A/C To* | 1200 ⌄ | Bank Current Account |
| Nominal Code* | 4904 ⌄ | Rent Income |

Recurring Entry Details

Transaction Type	Bank/Cash/Credit Card Receipt ⌄
Transaction Ref	STO
Transaction Details	Kieran Judson rent for storage
Department*	0 ⌄ Default

Posting Frequency

Every*	1 Month(s) ⌄	Total Required Postings	6
Start Date*	20/07/2016	Finish Date	20/12/2016
Next Posting Date	20/07/2016	Suspend Posting ?	☐
Last Posted			

Posting Amounts

Net Amount 200.00   Tax Code* T2 0.00 ⌄   VAT 0.00

OK   Cancel

Note the following:

- He inputs the bank account (1200) and the nominal code (4904)
- He chooses Bank/Cash/Credit Card Receipt

- The Transaction Ref is 'STO' (for Standing Order)
- The Transaction Details explain what the payment is for
- The posting frequency is once a month
- The start date is 20 July 2016
- The number of Total Required Postings is 6
- The Net Amount and VAT (Tax) Code (T2) are entered

Ross returns to the RECURRING ITEMS screen, which shows the two transactions.

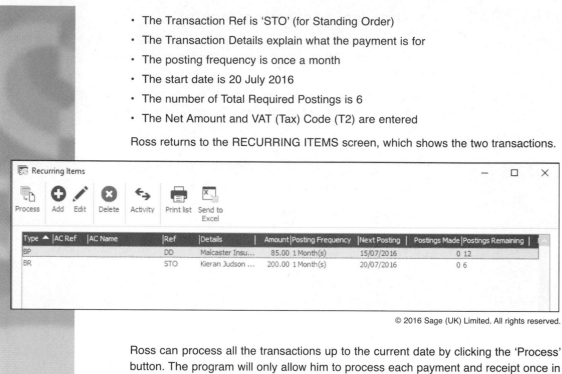

Ross can process all the transactions up to the current date by clicking the 'Process' button. The program will only allow him to process each payment and receipt once in each month.

Chapter Summary

- Businesses can set up accounts on a computer accounting program for funds of money held by the business. These accounts are classified as 'bank' accounts, but the money is not held at the bank. The money for these accounts will come from the bank or will be paid into the bank and recorded by a Bank Transfer.

- Accounts other than the Bank Current Account include:
  - Petty Cash Account – a cash fund held under lock and key in the office, used for small payments and receipts
  - Credit Card Account – records payments by employees on company credit cards

  These two accounts will be 'topped up' regularly by a transfer from the Bank Current Account.

- 'Bank' accounts for receiving payments may also be set up, for example a Cash Register account or a Card Receipts account. These record money received from sales and held in the business. When the money is paid into the Bank Current Account a Bank Transfer will be made on the computer.

- Businesses use Recurring Items on the computer accounting system to record regular payments made in and out of the Bank Current Account. These include standing orders and direct debits for outgoing payments and incoming receipts. The Recurring Items facility enables the business to set up the payments so that they can be recorded automatically.

Key Terms

petty cash	a float of cash kept in the office for making small purchases and receipts
petty cash account	an account used to record payments out of and receipts into the office petty cash fund
petty cash voucher	the document which records and authorises petty cash transactions
company credit card account	an account used to record payments made on credit cards issued to employees to cover business expenses
cash receipts account	an account used to record cash received by a business where the money is kept for a time by the business before it is paid into the bank
recurring entry	a bank payment or receipt which occurs on a regular basis and which is automated within the computer accounting program
Standing order/Direct debit schedule	a document which lists recurring payments and receipts with their due dates

Activities

9.1 What entries to the computer accounts are made when the Petty Cash system is operated for the following transactions? State which screens are used:

(a) for transfers into Petty Cash

(b) for payments out of Petty Cash

(c) for receipts into Petty Cash

9.2 You are getting some petty cash vouchers ready for input and notice some points which you think might cause problems:

(a) A petty cash voucher for postage stamps does not have any VAT shown on it.

(b) A petty cash voucher for stationery does not have any VAT shown on it.

(c) A petty cash voucher does not have an authorisation signature on it.

Write down what you think should be done in these three situations.

9.3 If a shop kept the cash and cheques taken from sales on the premises and only paid into the bank at the end of every week, it might use the Cash Register Account on the computer.

(a) Describe the entries the business would make on the Cash Register Account.

(b) Write down two disadvantages to the business of keeping money on the premises.

9.4 Describe the circumstances in which a business might set up Recurring Entries on the computer.

TAPPER TIMBER INPUTTING TASKS

Set the program date as 31 July 2016.

Task 1

On 1 July Ross drew £100 at his bank to top up the petty cash system.

Carry out a bank transfer from Bank Current Account to Petty Cash Account for this amount.

Task 2

Ross has just authorised two more petty cash vouchers (shown below). Input these together with the four petty cash vouchers on pages 133 to 134, taking particular care with the VAT element on each one (postage is VAT-exempt). Print out a Day Books: Cash Payments (Detailed) Report and a Day Books: Cash Receipts (Detailed) Report to confirm the accuracy of your input of the six vouchers (see p190). Hint: remember to select the Petty Cash Bank account on-screen before running the report.

The nominal code for Packaging is 5003.

---

petty cash voucher   Number *PC105*

                                   date   *28 July 2016*

description		amount	
		£	p
Receipt *Postage stamps*		3	15
	VAT	0	00
		3	15

signature *A McKay*

authorised *R Tapper*

---

petty cash voucher   Number *PC106*

                                   date   *28 July 2016*

description		amount	
		£	p
Payment *Packaging*		4	00
	VAT		80
Receipt obtained		4	80

signature *Nicky Smith*

authorised *Ross Tapper*

Task 3

(a)   Ross decides to start using the Cash Register account to record cash takings held in the safe before paying them into the bank. The details are:

Date	Details	Net amount £	VAT £	Total £	Reference*
15/07/16	Sheds cash sales	3,015.85	603.17	3,619.02	T001
15/07/16	Fencing cash sales	1,463.40	292.68	1,756.08	T002
22/07/16	Animal housing cash sales	604.00	120.80	724.80	T003
22/07/16	Garden furniture cash sales	5,921.05	1,184.21	7,105.26	T004
Totals		11,004.30	2,200.86	13,205.16	

*The reference is the cash till reference.

Enter these transactions, check the totals, SAVE and print out a Bank Receipts (Detailed) Day Book Report. Check with the printout on page 190.

(b)   Weekly totals are transferred from the Cash Register Account to the Bank Account. Enter the following transfers:

Date	Details	£	Paying in reference
18/07/16	From Cash Register to Bank	5,375.10	10740
25/07/16	From Cash Register to Bank	7,830.06	10741

Task 4

Create recurring entries for the payments and receipts listed on the schedule below. Be careful to note which transactions are payments and which are receipts and what the frequency is.

Use the following nominal codes:

7104 Premises Insurance; 4904 Rent income; 7103 General rates; 7801 Cleaning

Tapper Timber Standing Order and Direct Debit Schedule						
Start date	Type	To/From	Details	Value	Frequency	Total payments
15 July 2016	DD payment	Malcaster Insurance	Premises insurance	£85.00 (VAT exempt)	Monthly	12
20 July 2016	STO receipt	Kieran Judson	Rent for storage	£200.00 (VAT exempt)	Monthly	6
26 July 2016	STO payment	Stourcastle DC	Business rates	£350.00 (VAT exempt)	Monthly	7
29 July 2016	STO payment	Property Cleaning	Cleaning contract	£120.00 (£100 plus VAT)	Weekly	Indefinite (perpetual)

When the recurring entries have been set up process them for July.

Task 5

Print out a trial balance as at 31 July 2016. Check it against the one on page 191.

10 Reports and routines

this chapter covers...

■ One of the major advantages of running a computer accounting software is that it will provide the business manager and administrative staff with a wide range of reports – on demand.

■ These reports are produced regularly – sometimes at the end of the month – to enable the business to check the accuracy of its records and to ensure that customer and supplier payments are being made on time.

■ The reports that can be produced to help with checking the accuracy of the records include:
  – the trial balance – a full list of the General ledger account balances
  – the audit trail – a full numbered list of the transactions input on the computer in order of input

■ The reports that can be produced to help with dealing with customers and suppliers include:
  – 'aged' analyses – separate lists of customers and suppliers which show what payments are due and when
  – activity reports – lists of transactions on individual accounts
  – account lists – lists of customers and suppliers with telephone numbers
  – label lists – names and addresses of customers and suppliers – suitable for mailing labels
  – customer statements – sent to each sales ledger customer, listing transactions and telling the customer the amount that is due

■ A further regular checking routine is the bank reconciliation statement which agrees the bank statement with the accounting records of the business.

■ The end of the month is also a good time to process recurring entries and other regular account transfers.

■ The business in the Case Study – Tapper Timber – has reached the end of July and so will be used in this chapter to illustrate the various reports and routines and their uses.

THE IMPORTANCE OF INFORMATION

information for management

The accounting system of any business – whether hand-written or computer-based – contains important information for management and provides an accurate basis for decision-making. The advantage of using a computer accounting system is that this information is available instantly.

The **trial balance** is a list of the General ledger account balances at a set date – which is often the last day of the month. The figures are set out in balancing debit and credit columns to prove the accuracy of the bookkeeping entries. If the column totals are not the same in a manual system, there are likely to be errors in the double-entry bookkeeping. Computerised trial balances will normally balance.

The trial balance figures show how much money there is in the bank and provides management with details about sales and expense accounts.

Activity on individual accounts, eg sales, can be printed using a **nominal activity** report.

information for finance and administrative staff

The computer accounting program also enables finance and administrative staff to extract useful information, for example:

- The **audit trail** is a full list of the transactions input into the computer, presented in order of input. Accounts staff will use the audit trail to check the accuracy of the input and trace any discrepancies and errors.
- The analysis of customer accounts (the **aged debtors analysis**) tells credit control staff which customers need chasing for payment and which debts may need writing off. The computer can also print letters to customers chasing overdue accounts.
- The analysis of supplier accounts (the **aged creditors analysis**) tells accounts staff which bills and invoices need paying and when.
- The computer will also produce **activity reports** on individual customer and supplier accounts; these list all the transactions on each individual account and are useful to bring up on-screen when a customer telephones in with a query.
- Computer-produced **account lists** set out the names, account codes and telephone numbers of customers and suppliers. These are useful to sales and accounts staff when contacting customers and suppliers and when coding invoices and credit notes.
- The computer will also produce the names and addresses of customers and suppliers on **labels**, which is useful when doing a promotional mailing or a change of address notification.

We will now illustrate these procedures with a continuation of the Case Study.

Case
Study

TAPPER TIMBER:
END-OF-MONTH REPORTS

It is 31 July 2016. Ross Tapper has completed the input into his computer accounting system during the course of the month. Looking back he can see that he has:

- set up the company details and the General Ledger balances
- entered customer and supplier records and balances
- input customer and supplier invoices and credit notes processed during July
- input payments received from customers and sent to suppliers during July
- input cash receipts and payments for July
- set up a petty cash system and recurring entries for standing orders and direct debits

trial balance

Ross first extracts his trial balance as at the end of July. He does this by clicking on TRIAL BALANCE on the NOMINAL CODES toolbar. His printout is shown below.

Date: Time:	**Tapper Timber** **Period Trial Balance**		Page: 1
To Period:	Month 1, July 2016		

N/C	Name	Debit	Credit
0020	Plant and Machinery	17,490.00	
0030	Office Equipment	10,965.00	
0050	Motor Vehicles	17,995.00	
1001	Stock	18,467.18	
1100	Debtors Control Account	10,888.72	
1200	Bank Current Account	27,501.76	
1230	Petty Cash	49.23	
2100	Creditors Control Account		6,204.66
2200	Sales Tax Control Account		20,186.91
2201	Purchase Tax Control Account	13,301.73	
2300	Loans		31,303.80
3000	Capital		30,000.00
3050	Drawings	2,000.00	
4000	Sales - Fencing		5,308.70
4001	Sales - Garden furniture		12,801.60
4002	Sales - Sheds		14,276.35
4003	Sales - Animal housing		4,993.60
4904	Rent Income		200.00
5000	Materials Purchased	4,339.15	
5003	Packaging	4.00	
6201	Advertising	900.00	
7103	General Rates	350.00	
7104	Premises Insurance	85.00	
7501	Postage and Carriage	21.85	
7502	Office Stationery	13.00	
7550	Telephone and Fax	312.00	
7700	Equipment Hire	456.00	
7801	Cleaning	136.00	
	Totals:	125,275.62	125,275.62

The trial balance shows the balances of the General Ledger Accounts. The debit column on the left equals the credit column on the right because in double entry bookkeeping the total of debit entries should always equal the total of credit entries.

If in a manual accounting system the two columns totals were not the same, there could be one or more errors in the bookkeeping entries. In a computer-based system the totals should always be the same because the computer generates equal debits and credits from every entry.

audit trail

Ross regularly prints an audit trail as a further check (and also to satisfy his accountants). This shows each transaction entered into the computer in order of input. It is done from the AUDIT TRAIL REPORT icon on the TRANSACTIONS toolbar. An extract from a Detailed Audit Trail is shown below.

Date: **Tapper Timber**   **Page:** 1
Time: **Audit Trail (Detailed)**

Date From: 01/01/1980   **Customer From:**
Date To: 31/12/2019   **Customer To:** ZZZZZZZ

Transaction From: 32   **Supplier From:**
Transaction To: 40   **Supplier To:** ZZZZZZZZ

Exclude Deleted Tran: No

No	Type	A/C	N/C	Dept	Details	Date	Ref	Net	Tax	T/C	Pd	Paid	V	B	Bank Rec.
32	SI	VH001				14/07/2016	10028	1,138.60	227.72		N	0.00		-	
		32	4003	0	Kennels			1,138.60	227.72	T1		0.00	N		
33	SC	CS001				15/07/2016	553	140.00	28.00		N	0.00		-	
		33	4002	0	Overcharged tack shed			140.00	28.00	T1		0.00	N		
34	PI	ET001				05/07/2016	16-2941	1,549.30	309.86		N	0.00		-	
		34	5000	0	Posts and planks			1,549.30	309.86	T1		0.00	N		
35	PI	CP001				11/07/2016	7655	1,230.00	246.00		N	0.00		-	
		35	5000	0	Bow top panels			1,230.00	246.00	T1		0.00	N		
36	PI	JF001				12/07/2016	M42206	391.25	78.25		N	0.00		-	
		36	5000	0	Assorted fixings			391.25	78.25	T1		0.00	N		
37	PC	JF001				01/07/2016	R281	136.00	27.20		Y	163.20		-	
		37	5000	0	Post supports overcharged 163.20 to PI 6	01/07/2016	M41997	136.00	27.20	T1		163.20	N		
												163.20			
38	PC	CP001				06/07/2016	C93	225.00	45.00		Y	270.00		-	
		38	5000	0	Returned hurdles 270.00 to PI 4	06/07/2016	7611	225.00	45.00	T1		270.00	N		
												270.00			
39	PI	ET002				08/07/2016	9241	2,000.00	400.00		N	0.00		-	
		39	0020	0	Band saw			2,000.00	400.00	T1		0.00	N		
40	SR	OC001				08/07/2016	FP receipt	2,904.20	0.00		Y	2,904.20		N	
		40	1200	0	Sales Receipt 2904.20 to SI 1	08/07/2016	10013	2,904.20	0.00	T9		2,904.20	-		

Every transaction input into the computer (within the time period stipulated) is shown on the audit trail. The columns of the audit trail show, from the left:

1 the unique number allocated by the computer to the transaction

2 the type of transaction, for example SI = sales invoice, PI = purchase invoice

3 the account into which the item is entered

4 the Nominal code relating to the transaction

5 the Department reference, not used here

6 the description of the transaction. In the case of a sales receipt (SR) the allocation of the amount to specific transactions is shown

7 the date of the transaction (which is not necessarily the date of input)

8 the transaction reference (eg invoice number)

9 the net amount

10 any VAT

11 VAT tax code

12 whether paid

13 the gross ('paid') amount

14 whether the item is VAT reconciled, ie processed in a VAT Return

15 whether the item is bank reconciled (with the date)

Ross will need to keep the audit trail for future reference in case any errors or discrepancies come to light. His accountants may also need to see it if they have to verify his accounts.

nominal activity

Ross can check his monthly sales for each sales code. He selects code 4000 (Sales - Fencing) in the Nominal Codes screen and then clicks on REPORTS. In Nominal Activity Reports he chooses Nominal Activity and enters the date range of 1-31 July. The report, shown below, shows total fencing sales of £5,308.70 for the month.

Date:					**Tapper Timber**					Page:	1
Time:					**Nominal Activity**						

Date From:	01/07/2016							N/C From:	4000
Date To:	31/07/2016							N/C To:	4000

Transaction From: 1
Transaction To: 99,999,999

N/C:	4000		Name:	Fencing				Account Balance:		5,308.70 CR

No	Type	Date	Account	Ref	Details	Dept	T/C	Value	Debit	Credit	V	B
26	SI	05/07/2016	OC001	10024	Stock fencing	0	T1	658.25		658.25	N	-
29	SC	07/07/2016	OC001	552	Stock fencing damaged	0	T1	131.65	131.65		N	-
30	SI	11/07/2016	CS001	10026	Palisade fencing	0	T1	2,028.00		2,028.00	N	-
31	SI	12/07/2016	OC001	10027	5-bar gates	0	T1	425.00		425.00	N	-
54	BR	11/07/2016	1200	10738	Fencing cash sales	0	T1	865.70		865.70	N	N
69	BR	15/07/2016	1235	T002	Fencing cash sales	0	T1	1,463.40		1,463.40	N	-
							Totals:		131.65	5,440.35		
							History Balance:			5,308.70		

aged debtors analysis

It is important to Ross that he knows that his customers who buy on credit pay up on time. The credit period is indicated to them on the bottom of each invoice. Ross allows his customers 30 days from the date of the invoice in which to pay.

An Aged Debtors Analysis shows the amount owing by each customer and splits it up according to the length of time it has been outstanding. The Aged Debtors Analysis can be printed from the REPORTS icon on the CUSTOMERS toolbar. Alternatively an aged balance list can be produced from the AGED DEBT icon in CUSTOMERS.

Ross's Aged Debtors Analysis Report as at 31 July 2016 is shown below:

Date:		**Tapper Timber**						Page: 1		
Time:		**Aged Debtors Analysis (Summary)**								

Report Date:	31/07/2016								
Include future transactions:	No						Customer From:		
Exclude later payments:	No						Customer To:	ZZZZZZZZ	

** NOTE: All report values are shown in Base Currency, unless otherwise indicated **

A/C	Name	Credit Limit	Turnover	Balance	Future	Current	Period 1	Period 2	Period 3	Older
CS001	Cornwood Stud	£ 15,000.00	7,628.00	9,880.48	0.00	9,153.60	726.88	0.00	0.00	0.00
OC001	Oliver Cole & Sons	£ 5,000.00	951.60	-358.08	0.00	-358.08	0.00	0.00	0.00	0.00
VH001	Victoria Hotel	£ 15,000.00	3,338.60	1,366.32	0.00	1,366.32	0.00	0.00	0.00	0.00
	Totals:		11,918.20	10,888.72	0.00	10,161.84	726.88	0.00	0.00	0.00

The columns show (from left to right)

- the customer account number and name
- the credit limit (the maximum amount of credit Ross will allow on the account)
- the turnover (total net sales for each customer in the current financial year)
- the balance (the total balance on the customer's account)
- any transactions due in future months
- 'current' values are less than 30 days old; 'Period 1' values are 31-60 days old as at 31 July 2016

Note that the Report can be dated at any date required. Here it is dated 31 July.

The Report shows the following:

- All the accounts are trading within their credit limits (ie the figure in the 'Balance' column is less than the 'Credit Limit' column) – this is a good sign.
- The total of the Balance column shows that Tapper Timber is owed a total of £10,888.72 on 31 July. As a further check this figure could be agreed with the balance of Debtors Control Account on the trial balance (see page 150).

aged creditors analysis

Ross also needs to check on the amounts that Tapper Timber owes its Suppliers (creditors) for goods purchased, and to make sure that there are no amounts outstanding for longer than they should be. The Aged Creditors Analysis enables him to do this. It can be printed from REPORTS on the SUPPLIERS toolbar. The layout of the columns works on the same principles as the Aged Debtors Analysis (see above). Alternatively the AGED BALANCES icon in SUPPLIERS can also be used to produce a list of amounts due to suppliers.

A/C	Name	Credit Limit	Turnover	Balance	Future	Current	Period 1	Period 2	Period 3	Older

Date: Tapper Timber **Page:** 1
Time: **Aged Creditors Analysis (Summary)**

Report Date: 31/07/2016   Supplier From:
Include future transactions: No   Supplier To: ZZZZZZZZ
Exclude Later Payments: No

** NOTE: All report values are shown in Base Currency, unless otherwise indicated **

A/C	Name	Credit Limit	Turnover	Balance	Future	Current	Period 1	Period 2	Period 3	Older
CP001	Chapman Panels	£ 15,000.00	1,005.00	1,476.00	0.00	1,476.00	0.00	0.00	0.00	0.00
ET001	Estate Timber Ltd	£ 7,500.00	1,549.30	1,859.16	0.00	1,859.16	0.00	0.00	0.00	0.00
ET002	Emery Tools Ltd	£ 5,000.00	2,000.00	2,400.00	0.00	2,400.00	0.00	0.00	0.00	0.00
JF001	Johnsons Fixings	£ 15,000.00	255.25	469.50	0.00	469.50	0.00	0.00	0.00	0.00
	Totals:		4,809.55	6,204.66	0.00	6,204.66	0.00	0.00	0.00	0.00

This report shows that:

- Tapper Timber is up-to-date with payments to suppliers – all amounts due are 'current', ie there is nothing outstanding for more than 30 days.
- The total owed by Tapper Timber is £6,204.66 on 31 July. As a further check this figure should be agreed with the balance of Creditors Control Account on the trial balance (see page 150).

customer activity reports

Ross receives a call from Nicola Ashby at Cornwood Stud. Nicola has not yet received a statement of account and wants to find out what is outstanding. Ross needs to bring up this account on-screen; he can do this by clicking on the ACTIVITY icon on the CUSTOMERS toolbar with the appropriate account selected. The screen can be printed if required.

Alternatively Ross could select the account on the CUSTOMERS screen and click on the REPORTS icon to select the Customer Activity (Summary) Report, allowing the default date range. The report shows that there is a total of £9,880.48 outstanding on the account. This is made up of the balance of invoice 10019, £726.88; invoice 10025, £6,888.00; invoice 10026, £2,433.60 less credit note 553, £168.00. Items marked with a 'p' are part paid; items marked with an asterisk are outstanding.

Date: Tapper Timber **Page:** 1
Time: **Customer Activity (Summary)**

Date From: 01/01/1980   Customer From: CS001
Date To: 31/07/2016   Customer To: CS001
Inc b/fwd transaction: No   Transaction From: 1
Exc later payment: No   Transaction To: 99,999,999

** NOTE: All report values are shown in Base Currency, unless otherwise indicated **

A/C: CS001   Name: Cornwood Stud   Contact: Nicola Ashby   Tel: 01908 674237

No	Items	Type	Date	Ref	Details	Value	O/S	Debit	Credit
3	1	SI	24/06/2016	10019	Opening Balance	5,726.88 p	726.88	5,726.88	
27	1	SI	07/07/2016	10025	Tack shed	6,888.00 *	6,888.00	6,888.00	
30	1	SI	11/07/2016	10026	Palisade fencing	2,433.60 *	2,433.60	2,433.60	
33	1	SC	15/07/2016	553	Overcharged tack shed	168.00 *	-168.00		168.00
42	1	SR	22/07/2016	FP receipt	Sales Receipt	5,000.00	0.00		5,000.00
						9,880.48	9,880.48	15,048.48	5,168.00

Amount Outstanding 9,880.48
Amount Paid this period 5,000.00
Credit Limit £ 15,000.00

other useful reports

Ross has also printed a Customer List from his computer; this is an alphabetically sorted account list of customers, together with their contact numbers. A similar report – Customer Address List – produces customer addresses. These reports can be accessed from REPORTS in CUSTOMERS.

Tapper Timber
Customer List

Customer From:
Customer To: ZZZZZZZZ

Show Active/Inactive: Active and Inactive(*)

A/C	Name	Contact Name	Telephone	Fax
CS001	Cornwood Stud	Nicola Ashby	01908 674237	
OC001	Oliver Cole & Sons	Dan Cole	01908 824295	
VH001	Victoria Hotel	Sana Roy	01908 345287	

The same exercise can be carried out from the SUPPLIERS toolbar to produce a list of Suppliers with contact numbers.

The computer will also enable Ross to print out name and address labels for Customers and Suppliers. This could be very useful when marketing products to Customers – sending out a catalogue, for example. The labels can be printed by clicking on the LABELS icon on the CUSTOMERS or SUPPLIERS toolbar and selecting an appropriate label format. The labels shown below are extracted from Ross's Customer details printed as Laser Sales Labels (A4).

Nicola Ashby	Dan Cole	Sana Roy
Cornwood Stud	Oliver Cole & Sons	Victoria Hotel
The Foal Yard	Wood Farm	67 The Parade
Bartisham	Collingwood	Stourcastle
ST6 4KG	ST8 6TF	ST4 6HG

customer statements

At the end of each month Ross will print out statements and send them to his customers. This can be done from the STATEMENT icon on the CUSTOMERS toolbar. A suitable format can then be chosen from the list shown on the screen. At this point Ross could choose to email statements to his customers using the Email option in the Preview screen. The statements set out the transactions on the Customer account and state the amount owing. Statements are important documents because some customers will pay from the monthly statement rather than the invoice.

The statement for Cornwood Stud is shown on the next page.

Tapper Timber
Unit 3
Greenslade Way
Stourcastle
ST4 6TG

Tel : 01877 453611
Email : info@tappertimber.co.uk

STATEMENT

Date	31/07/2016
Account Ref	CS001

Cornwood Stud
The Foal Yard

Bartisham

ST6 4KG

All values are shown in Pound Sterling

Date	Ref	Details	Debit	Credit	Balance
24/06/2016	10019	Opening Balance	5,726.88		5,726.88
07/07/2016	10025	Tack shed	6,888.00		12,614.88
11/07/2016	10026	Palisade fencing	2,433.60		15,048.48
15/07/2016	553	Overcharged tack shed		168.00	14,880.48
22/07/2016	FP receipt	Sales Receipt		5,000.00	9,880.48

	Current	Period 1	Period 2	Period 3	Older		Amount Due
£	9,153.60	£ 726.88	£ 0.00	£ 0.00	£ 0.00	£	9,880.48

BANK RECONCILIATION ON THE COMPUTER

the reasons for bank reconciliation

A further routine carried out on a regular basis, with the help of the computer accounting system, is the task of comparing and agreeing the entries in the bank current account for a set period of time, eg a month, and the entries on the actual bank statement for the same period. This process is known as **bank reconciliation**. It reconciles:

- the bank statement – what the bank states the balance actually is with…
- the bank account of a business – the balance representing what the accounting records of the business states it has in the bank

It is quite common that **differences** will arise and that the two amounts will not be the same.

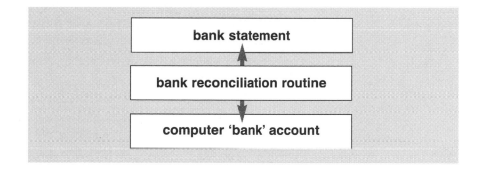

timing differences

These variations can arise from **timing differences**.

For example, a cheque that is issued by the business and sent off to a supplier will be input into the computer accounting records of the business when it is issued, but will not yet have been paid in at the bank by the supplier. Consequently the bank balance on the computer of the business writing the cheque will differ by this amount from the bank balance of the business shown on the bank statement - until, of course, the cheque is paid in and eventually deducted from the bank account. This is a 'timing difference'.

Another timing difference will occur when cheques received from customers of a business have been entered into the bank account on the computer but are still waiting to be paid into the bank on a paying-in slip. The accounting records of the business will show that the money has gone into the bank account, but the actual bank statement will only show the increase after the cheques have been paid into the bank, possibly a day or two later.

Also, there may be items on the bank statement which the business will not immediately know about and will need to enter into the accounting records **after** it has received the bank statement. Examples are bank charges, bank interest paid and bank interest received.

bank reconciliation in Sage

As seen on the previous page, bank reconciliation forms a link between the balances shown in the bank statement and in the accounting records of the business. All the reconciliation is doing in effect is explaining what items make up the difference between the bank statement and the bank account in the accounting records of the business.

The Bank Reconciliation process, accessed through RECONCILE in BANK ACCOUNTS, is illustrated in the Case Study which follows. The procedure is:

1 In the statement summary screen enter a statement reference (optional), the closing balance on the bank statement and the bank statement date. Any interest earned or bank charges can be added at this point. Click OK to move to the main Bank Reconciliation screen.

2 Check that the Matched Balance box at the bottom agrees to the opening balance on the bank statement.

3 Compare the items in the upper window on the screen with the bank statement. Click to select any items that appear on both, then click the Match button to transfer the matched item/s to the lower window. Alternatively double-click the matched items individually to transfer them.

4 Update the computer with any items appearing on the bank statement but not in Sage by inputting them using the 'Adjust' button.

5 When you have transferred all the matched items to the lower screen and made any adjustments, check that the Statement Balance equals the bank statement closing balance and the Difference box shows zero.

6 Click 'Reconcile'.

Now read the Case Study which follows.

TAPPER TIMBER:
BANK RECONCILIATION ROUTINE

It is 31 July 2016. Ross has printed out an online bank statement which is shown below.

ALBION BANK PLC

Statement of account as at: 31 07 2016

Account 90 47 17 11719881 Tapper Timber

Date	Description		Paid in	Paid out	Balance
01-Jul	Balance b/f				13210.58
01-Jul	Cash withdrawal	D/card		100.00	13110.58
04-Jul	Cash	10736	5616.66		18727.24
04-Jul	Cash	10737	3901.20		22628.44
06-Jul	Cheque	122992		1835.52	20792.92
07-Jul	Timber magazine	D/Card		1080.00	19712.92
08-Jul	Cole	FP rec	2904.20		22617.12
08-Jul	R Tapper	FP pay		2000.00	20617.12
11-Jul	Cash	10738	1038.84		21655.96
11-Jul	Cash	10739	6792.60		28448.56
13-Jul	ST Telecom	FP pay		374.40	28074.16
15-Jul	Paid in	Cheque	9900.78		37974.94
15-Jul	Malcaster Ins	DD		85.00	37889.94
18-Jul	Chapman	FP pay		5972.52	31917.42
18-Jul	Davies Hire	D/card		547.20	31370.22
18-Jul	Paid in	10740	5375.10		36745.32
20-Jul	Judson	SO rec	200.00		36945.32
22-Jul	Cornwood	FP rec	5000.00		41945.32
22-Jul	Estate Timber	FP pay		4506.00	37439.32
25-Jul	Paid in	10741	7830.06		45269.38
26-Jul	Johnsons	FP pay		4843.62	40425.76
26-Jul	Stourcastle DC	SO pay		350.00	40075.76
29-Jul	Prop Clg	SO pay		120.00	39955.76
31-Jul	O Cole	FP rec	1500.00		41455.76
31-Jul	Bank charges			50.00	41405.76

He wants to carry out a reconciliation routine and so he opens the BANK ACCOUNTS module and selects the Bank Current Account. Then he clicks RECONCILE.

He compares the bank statement with the computer screen.

- He completes the Statement Summary screen with a Statement Reference (he uses the date), the bank statement ending balance (£41,405.76) and the statement date (31 July 2016). He clicks OK to move to the main reconciliation screen.

- He checks that the opening balance of £13,210.58 on the bank statement is the same as the Matched Balance on the screen. It is.

- He selects each item in the upper window that is also on the bank statement. He can use the scroll bar to move up and down or he can change the size of the upper and lower windows by dragging on the horizontal bar between them.

- Now he clicks the Match button to transfer the matched transactions to the lower window.

Reconcile - 1200 - Bank Current Account

View history | Report | Print list | Send to Excel

Statement reference: 31 07 16 | End date: 31/07/2016 | End balance: 41405.76

Un-matched transactions

Date	No.	Reference	Details	Payments	Receipts
27/07/2016	58	Cheque	Ross Tapper capital		5000.00
29/07/2016	59	122993	Delivery vehicle	21594.00	
31/07/2016	48	Cheque	Sales Receipt		2640.00

Find... | Swap | Clear | 0.00 | Match >>

Date	No.	Reference	Details	Payments	Receipts	Balance
		O/Bal	Last reconciled balance			13210.58
01/07/2016	51	122992	Materials purchased	1835.52		11375.06
01/07/2016	60	TRANS	From bank to petty cash	100.00		11275.06
04/07/2016	49	10736	Garden furniture cash sa...		5616.66	16891.72
04/07/2016	50	10737	Animal housing cash sales		3901.20	20792.92
07/07/2016	52	Debit card	Advertising	1080.00		19712.92
08/07/2016	40	FP receipt	Sales Receipt		2904.20	22617.12
08/07/2016	53	Faster pa...	Drawings	2000.00		20617.12
11/07/2016	54	10738	Fencing cash sales		1038.84	21655.96
11/07/2016	55	10739	Sheds cash sales		6792.60	28448.56

<< Unmatch | 0.00 | Swap | Clear | Adjust...

Matched transactions

Book Balance	Total Payments	Total Receipts	Matched Balance	Statement Balance	Difference
27501.76	21814.26	50059.44	41455.76	41405.76	50.00

Save progress | Reconcile | Close

- There is a figure of £50 in the difference box. This is the Bank charges which have not yet been entered. Ross clicks on the 'Adjust' button and then chooses Bank Payment. He now enters a payment for the charges in the normal way. The nominal code is 7901 and the VAT code is T2. He then hits Save.

Bank Payments

Clear form | Print Cheque | Insert row (F7) | Remove row (F8) | Copy cell above (F6) | Copy cell above +1 (Shift + F6) | Calculate net (F9) | Memorise | Recall | Print list | Send to Excel

Bank: Bank Current Account | Tax Rate: 0.00
N/C: Bank Charges | Total: 50.00

Bank*	Date*	Ref	Ex.Ref	N/C*	Departmen	Project Ref	Cost Code	Details	Net	T/C*	Tax
1200	31/07/2016	Bank		7901	0			Bank charges	50.00	T2	0.00

| | | | | | | | | | 50.00 | | 0.00 |

Save | Close

- Finally, Ross is returned to the Bank Reconciliation screen where he checks that the Difference box is now showing zero.

All the unmatched (ie 'unreconciled') items on the screen will appear next time the routine is carried out.

By carrying out this routine, Ross can make sure that he has entered all his bank transactions correctly, and that the bank has not made any errors.

Before closing the Reconcile screen, Ross clicks the 'Report' button at the top of the screen to print a Bank Reconciliation report.

```
Date:  29/03/2016                    Tapper Timber           Page:  1
Time:  15:19:30                     Bank Reconciliation

  Bank Ref:    1200                      Date To:       31/07/2016
  Bank Name:   Bank Current Account      Statement Ref: 1200 2016-07-31 02
  Currency:    Pound Sterling

Balance as per cash book at 31/07/2016:                        27,451.76

Add: Unpresented Payments

    Tran No    Date        Ref      Details                  £

      59       29/07/2016  122993   Delivery vehicle      21,594.00
                                                          _____
                                                          21,594.00

Less: Outstanding Receipts

    Tran No    Date        Ref      Details                  £

      48       31/07/2016  Cheque   Sales Receipt          2,640.00
      58       27/07/2016  Cheque   R Tapper capital       5,000.00
                                                          _____
                                                          (7,640.00)

Reconciled balance :                                       41,405.76

Balance as per statement :                                 41,405.76

Difference :                                                    0.00

                                    © 2016 Sage (UK) Limited. All rights reserved.
```

Now he can click 'Reconcile' to complete the task.

OTHER MONTH-END ROUTINES

It is important for a business with a computer accounting system to establish an end-of-month routine which includes the production of the reports illustrated in the Case Studies in this chapter. Examples of other month-end routines involving the computer accounting system are explained below.

checking that all transactions have been input

The business must check that all the necessary transactions – sales and purchases transactions, payments made and received – have been input into the computer before extracting the reports.

recurring entries

Recurring entries – standing orders and direct debits – may be processed monthly, and it should become part of the month-end routine to ensure that this is done. Recurring entries are dealt with in detail on pages 139 to 142.

SCREENSHOTS

An image of the screen can be 'exported' to another program using the 'Print Scr' button on the keyboard. The image is held in the computer's memory until it is pasted into another program, eg Word. It can then be saved and given a suitable filename.

Such images are useful for demonstration purposes (they have been used extensively in this publication) and in a training environment where the student needs to show, or print a copy of, something that appeared on-screen.

Chapter Summary

- A computer accounting system has the advantage that it can provide a wide range of printed reports quickly. These are useful both for the management of the business and also for accounts staff.

- Reports can be produced to help with checking the accuracy of the records. These are often produced at the end of each month and include:
  - the trial balance – a full list of the General ledger balances
  - the audit trail – a numbered list of transactions set out in order of input on the computer

- Reports can be produced to help with day-to-day dealings with customers and suppliers. Month-end reports include:
  - 'aged' analyses – separate lists of customers and suppliers which show when payments are due and if any payments are overdue
  - activity reports – lists of transactions on individual accounts which need to be looked into
  - customer statements of account

- Other day-to-day useful printouts include customer and supplier account lists and label lists – useful for mailing purposes.

- Another regular routine is the bank reconciliation, which agrees the entries on the actual bank statement with those in the bank account records of the organisation.

- The end-of-month is the time to process recurring entries and other regular account transfers.

Key Terms		
	trial balance	a list of General ledger account balances set out in debit and credit columns, the totals of which should be the same
	audit trail	a numbered list of transactions on the computer produced in order of input
	aged debtors analysis	a list of customer balances which are split up according to the length of time they have been outstanding
	aged creditors analysis	a list of supplier balances which are split up according to the length of time they have been outstanding
	activity report	a list of transactions on individual Nominal, Customer and Supplier accounts
	bank reconciliation	the process of checking the bank statement entries against the accounting records of an organisation and identifying the differences that exist between the two documents

Activities

10.1 What is the purpose of a trial balance in a manual accounting system?

10.2 Why should the debit and credit columns in a trial balance add up to the same total when a computer accounting system is used?

10.3 What else does a trial balance tell the owner of a business?

10.4 An audit trail is a numbered list of transactions input into a computer accounting system. How is it set out – in date order or in order of input?

10.5 What is the main purpose of:

(a) an Aged Debtors Analysis?

(b) an Aged Creditors Analysis?

10.6 The Aged Debtors Analysis of Tapper Timber as at 31 July 2016 is shown below. Tapper Timber allows customers to pay up to 30 days from the date of the invoice.

(a) What is the total amount owed by the customers of Tapper Timber?

(b) Against which figure in the trial balance (see next page) should this total in (a) be checked?

(c) Suppose that in two months time the balance of Victoria Hotel's account still stood at £1,366.32 and this figure appeared in the 'Period 2' column. What does this tell Ross about the account? What other document could Ross print out to give him – and the customer – more information?

Date:								Page:	1	
Time:		**Tapper Timber**								
		Aged Debtors Analysis (Summary)								

Report Date: 31/07/2016   **Customer From:**
Include future transactions: No   **Customer To:**   ZZZZZZZZ
Exclude later payments: No

** NOTE: All report values are shown in Base Currency, unless otherwise indicated **

A/C	Name	Credit Limit	Turnover	Balance	Future	Current	Period 1	Period 2	Period 3	Older
CS001	Cornwood Stud	£ 15,000.00	7,628.00	9,880.48	0.00	9,153.60	726.88	0.00	0.00	0.00
OC001	Oliver Cole & Sons	£ 5,000.00	951.60	-358.08	0.00	-358.08	0.00	0.00	0.00	0.00
VH001	Victoria Hotel	£ 15,000.00	3,338.60	1,366.32	0.00	1,366.32	0.00	0.00	0.00	0.00
	Totals:		11,918.20	10,888.72	0.00	10,161.84	726.88	0.00	0.00	0.00

10.7 The trial balance (extract) of Tapper Timber at the close of business on 31 July 2016 is shown below. Study the figures and answer the questions that follow.

Date:		Tapper Timber	Page: 1
Time:		**Period Trial Balance**	

To Period: Month 1, July 2016

N/C	Name	Debit	Credit
0020	Plant and Machinery	17,490.00	
0030	Office Equipment	10,965.00	
0050	Motor Vehicles	17,995.00	
1001	Stock	18,467.18	
1100	Debtors Control Account	10,888.72	
1200	Bank Current Account	27,501.76	
1230	Petty Cash	49.23	
2100	Creditors Control Account		6,204.66
2200	Sales Tax Control Account		20,186.91
2201	Purchase Tax Control Account	13,301.73	
2300	Loans		31,303.80
3000	Capital		30,000.00
3050	Drawings	2,000.00	
4000	Sales - Fencing		5,308.70
4001	Sales - Garden furniture		12,801.60
4002	Sales - Sheds		14,276.35
4003	Sales - Animal housing		4,993.60
4904	Rent Income		200.00
5000	Materials Purchased	4,339.15	
5003	Packaging	4.00	
6201	Advertising	900.00	
7103	General Rates	350.00	
7104	Premises Insurance	85.00	
7501	Postage and Carriage	21.85	
7502	Office Stationery	13.00	
7550	Telephone and Fax	312.00	
7700	Equipment Hire	456.00	
7801	Cleaning	136.00	
	Totals:	125,275.62	125,275.62

(a) How much money has the company got in the bank?

(b) How much money has the company got stored on the premises?

(c) What is the company's total sales income (excluding rent) for the period up to 31 July?

TAPPER TIMBER INPUTTING TASKS

Set the program date to 31 July 2016.

Task 1

Print a Nominal Activity report for account number 4000 for the month of July. Check it against the one on page 192.

Task 2

Following the procedure on pages 159 to 163, carry out a bank reconciliation from RECONCILE in BANK ACCOUNTS.

Print a Bank Reconciliation Report before proceeding to Reconcile. Check the report against the one in the Case Study on page 163.

Task 3

Print an Audit Trail (Detailed) for any transactions dated 31 July. Check it against the one on page 192.

Task 4

Back up your data and take a screenshot of the completed back-up screen. Check it against the one on page 193.

11 Corrections and adjustments

this chapter covers...

■ When you are operating a computer accounting program it is inevitable that errors will be made. These might be your own input errors or they might be errors on the part of a customer or a supplier. Whatever the source of the error might be, it will have to be put right.

■ You can delete a transaction completely, or you can edit details on invoices, credit notes and payments. Editing is most commonly used for internal corrections – before any documents are sent out of the business.

■ The JOURNAL function is used for transferring amounts from one General ledger account to another. One of its uses is therefore for correcting mistakes where the wrong Nominal Code number has been used. A knowledge of the use of debits and credits is needed for the JOURNAL.

■ The computer also allows you to make adjustments to the records, for example:
   – you may need to 'write off' a customer account because you consider you will never get the money – the customer may have become bankrupt, for example

■ A customer cheque may be returned unpaid by the customer's bank.

CORRECTIONS

You will be able to correct or amend most input errors using the EDIT option on the TRANSACTIONS module toolbar.

You highlight the transaction that needs correcting (see screen below) and click on EDIT to bring up the screen shown at the bottom of the page. Here a change of the reference number is being made on the screen.

1

essional - Tapper Timber

dules   Settings   Tools   Favourites   WebLinks   Help

Audit trail   Accounts   Verification   Edit   Unallocate   Delete   Send to   Reports
report   audit   reports   Excel

Select the transaction and click Edit

Filter   Find   Search...   🔍 ⊘   All records (80)

No ▲	Type	Account	Nominal	Dept	Project	Details	Date	Posted Date	Ref	Ex.Ref	Net
26	SI	OC001	4000	0		Stock fencing	05/07/2016	12/01/2016	10024		658.25
27	SI	CS001	4002	0		Tack shed	07/07/2016	12/01/2016	10025		5740.00
28	SC	VH001	4001	0		Garden furniture missing	05/07/2016	12/01/2016	551		200.00
29	SC	OC001	4000	0		Stock fencing damaged	07/07/2016	12/01/2016	552		131.65
30	SI	CS001	4000	0		Palisade fencing	11/07/2016	12/01/2016	10026		2028.00
31	SI	OC001	4000	0		5-bar gates	12/07/2016	12/01/2016	10027		425.00
32	SI	VH001	4003	0		Kennels	14/07/2016	12/01/2016	10028		1138.60
33	SC	CS001	4002	0		Overcharged tack shed	15/07/2016	12/01/2016	553		140.00
34	PI	FT001	5000	0		Posts and planks	05/07/2016	12/01/2016	16-2941		1549.30
35	PI	CP001	5000	0		Bow top panels	11/07/2016	12/01/2016	7655		1230.00

2

Number 34, Purchase Invoice

You can change details of all grouped items at once by using the fields below, or select individual transactions in the list to amend a specific item.

Purchase Invoice Details

Account   ET001 ⌄

Amend the reference number here

Reference   16-2491

Description   Posts and planks   Posted by   MANAGER

Created on   05/07/2016   Edited by

Posted on   12/01/2016

Edited on   / /   VAT Rec. Date   / /

Net   1549.30   Paid   0.00

Tax   309.86

Currency   1 Pound Sterling ⌄   Foreign gross   1859.16

Exchange rate   1.000000

☐ Paid in full   ☐ Finance charge   ☐ Disputed   ☐ Printed
☐ Opening balance   ☐ CIS reconciled   ☐ Re-valuation

Item Line Details

No	N/C	Details	Net	T/C	Tax
34	5000	Posts and planks	1549.30	T1	309.86

Click here to make further amendments

To edit details of a specific item on...   nd click 'Edit'.   Edit

How will this affect my data?   Save   Close

3

Number 34, Purchase Invoice

Purchase Invoice Details

N/C   5000 ⌄

Details   Posts and planks

Date   05/07/2016

Nominal code can be changed

Department*   0 ⌄

Ex.Ref

Project Ref   ⌄   Cost Code   ⌄

Net   1549.30   T/C   T1 20.00 ⌄

Tax   309.86   Paid   0.00

☐ Paid in full   ☐ Disputed

Payment Allocations

Type	Date	Payment Ref	Details	Amount

Edit

Close

The screen labelled '2' on the previous page allows correction of:

- the account to which the invoice is posted
- the product description
- the reference and date

Further amendments (screen '3' on the previous page) can be made to an individual item highlighted in the bottom box by clicking 'Edit'. These include:

- the nominal code
- details
- the amounts charged
- the VAT rate and VAT amount

To delete a transaction in full, select it in the TRANSACTIONS module and click DELETE on the toolbar. The full transaction will be displayed. Click DELETE at the bottom of the screen to complete the operation.

JOURNAL ENTRIES

Journal entries are transfers from one General Ledger account to another. They may be used to make an accounting adjustment or to correct an inputting error.

In manual accounting, journals are used for unusual or irregular transactions. Here are some examples:

- entry of opening General Ledger account balances
- correction of a wrong ledger entry (sometimes called a 'misposting')
- writing off a customer account balance
- entering details of a returned customer cheque
- posting of depreciation of fixed assets*
- posting of accruals and prepayments*

*these are Advanced (Level 3) Accounting topics

journals and double entry

You need to be confident about **double-entry** bookkeeping and using debits and credits when doing journal entries. You will have to decide which accounts have debit entries and which accounts have credit entries. The rule is that for every transaction there are balancing debit and credit entries:

debits	=	money paid into the bank
		purchases and expenses
		an increase in an asset
credits	=	payments out of the bank
		sales and income
		an increase in a liability

If you are still in any doubt about debits and credits, use EDIT wherever possible to adjust account entries.

example

Suppose you were inputting a batch of Bank Payments which included a number of bills that had to be paid. You have paid £960 (£800 + VAT) to RPower for a gas bill, but when inputting it you thought it was for electricity and so posted it to electricity (nominal code 7200) instead of gas (7201).

The journal to correct the misposting is laid out in manual accounting as shown on the next page.

Journal entry 42 18 July 2016	Dr	Cr
Gas	800.00	
Electricity		800.00
Correction of misposting		

the solution

You could either use EDIT, but as you are a double-entry expert you choose to correct your mistake using a journal entry. You bring up the screen by clicking on the JOURNAL ENTRY icon on the NOMINAL CODES toolbar:

The procedure is:

- enter your reference
- enter the nominal code of the account to which you are going to post the debit; here it is Gas Account because you are recording an expense
- enter the reason for the transaction – here you are adjusting a misposting
- enter the VAT tax code input on the original (wrong) entry
- enter the net amount in the debit column (ie the amount before VAT has been added on) – here the net amount is £800 and VAT (assumed here at standard rate) is £160 and the total is £960; note that neither the VAT nor the total appear on the screen because you are not adjusting the VAT; *only the net amount* has gone to the wrong account

then on the next line…

- enter the nominal code of the account to which you are going to post the credit; here it is Electricity Account because you are effectively refunding the amount to the account – it is an income item and so a credit
- enter the remaining data as you did for the debit, but enter the net amount in the right-hand credit column
- make sure the Balance box reads zero – meaning that the debit equals the credit – and SAVE

ADJUSTMENTS TO THE ACCOUNTS

A business may from time-to-time need to make adjustments to the data which has already been input into the computer accounting system. Situations where this happens include:

- A credit customer is going or has gone 'bust' (bankrupt) and cannot pay invoices – the account will need to be 'written off' as irrecoverable

- a cheque paid to the business by a credit customer has 'bounced' – it has been returned by the bank after it has been paid in and the money is taken off the account of the business by the bank

We will look at each of the procedures in turn.

write offs

All businesses from time-to-time will encounter irrecoverable or bad debts. A **bad debt** is a credit customer who does not pay. It may be that the customer has gone 'bust' or that the cost of continuing to send statements, reminders and demands is too high in relation to the amount owing. A business will decide in these circumstances to **write off** the debt in the accounts. This involves:

- debiting 'Bad Debt Write off'

- crediting the customer with the amount due – wiping it off their account

In Sage this transfer is carried out through the WRITE OFFS option on the CUSTOMERS toolbar. This brings up the Write Off, Refund and Returns Wizard which gives a choice of accounting adjustments:

Screens then follow which allow the business to select the outstanding invoices to write off (all of them if the whole account is being written off) and then to date and confirm the details.

After this procedure the customer account will show as a nil balance and a corresponding Bad Debt Write Off account will show the write off amount as an expense to the business. The Debtors Control Account value will also be decreased by the amount of the write off. Eventually a write off – like any expense – will reduce the business profits.

adjusting for returned cheques

A **returned cheque** is a cheque which has been received by a business and paid in but returned by the cheque issuer's bank. There may be a lack of funds, or the cheque may have been stopped, or it may be technically incorrect (eg unsigned by the customer).

The appropriate computer accounting entries in Sage will be made through the Write off, Refunds and Returns Wizard under WRITE OFFS in CUSTOMERS. Customer Cheque Returns is first selected. The next screen is shown below.

Write Off, Refunds and Returns					✕

Write Off, Refund and Returns

1. Select Area
2. Process Data
3. Update Data
4. Post Data

Process Data

Select the cheque(s) you want to return from the list below

No	Bank	Date	Ref	Details	Amount
41	1200	15/07/2016	Cheque	Sales Receipt	9900.78
48	1200	31/07/2016	Cheque	Sales Receipt	2640.00

Swap | Clear

Cancel | Back | Next

In this example a cheque for £2,640.00 has been returned.

TAPPER TIMBER:
CORRECTIONS AND ADJUSTMENTS

It is 31 July 2016. Ross is finalising his month's accounts. There are some corrections to be made.

incorrect invoice number

A purchase invoice from Estate Timber has been entered as number 16-2941. It should have been 16-2491.

Ross identifies the invoice in the Transactions module. It is transaction 34.

He clicks EDIT and amends the invoice entry in the 'Reference' field.

He clicks SAVE and YES when asked 'Do you wish to post these changes?'

Number 34, Purchase Invoice		✕

You can change details of all grouped items at once by using the fields below, or select individual transactions in the list to amend a specific item.

Purchase Invoice Details

Account	ET001 ▾		Due on	04/08/2016

He amends the reference number here

Reference	16-2491			
Description	Posts and planks		Posted by	MANAGER
Created on	05/07/2016		Edited by	
Posted on	12/01/2016			
Edited on	/ /		VAT Rec. Date	/ /
Net	1549.30		Paid	0.00
Tax	309.86			
Currency	1 Pound Sterling ▾		Foreign gross	1859.16
Exchange rate	1.000000			

☐ Paid in full   ☐ Finance charge   ☐ Disputed   ☐ Printed
☐ Opening balance   ☐ CIS reconciled   ☐ Revaluation

Item Line Details

No	N/C	Details	Net	T/C	Tax
34	5000	Posts and planks	1549.30	T1	309.86

To edit details of a specific item on this Purchase Invoice, highlight the item and click 'Edit'. | Edit |

How will this affect my data?			Save	Close

journal entries

Cash sales for Animal Housing entered on 11 July have been wrongly coded as Sheds. The amount is £1,440.00 (£1,200 plus £240 VAT).

Ross prepares a journal entry as shown below to transfer the value to the correct Sales account.

Journal entry 15 31 July 2016	Dr	Cr
Sales - Sheds	1,200.00	
Sales - Animal Housing		1,200.00
Correction of misposting		

In double-entry terms this means:

Debit Sales - Sheds (code 4002) – reducing the income in that account

Credit Sales - Animal Housing (code 4003) – increasing the income in that account

Ross accesses the Journal screen through the JOURNALS ENTRY icon on the NOMINAL CODES toolbar. The journal screen after input appears as follows:

Note that:

- No VAT is involved here because it is only the net amount (amount before VAT is added on) that has gone to the wrong account

- The reference used is Jnl15, the next consecutive number in Ross's journal list

- The Balance box shows as zero because the debit entry equals the credit entry – as you would expect (the Balance is the difference between the entries)

Ross can keep a printed record of his journals by going to REPORTS in the NOMINAL CODES module and printing Day Books: General Ledger. In the criteria values screen he enters a date range of 31 July.

No	Type	N/C	Date	Ref	Ex.Ref	Details	Dept	T/C	Debit	Credit	V	B
81	JD	4002	31/07/2016	Jnl15		Correction of posting error	0	T1	1,200.00		N	-
82	JC	4003	31/07/2016	Jnl15		Correction of posting error	0	T1		1,200.00	N	-
								Totals:	1,200.00	1,200.00		

Date: Time:
Tapper Timber
Day Books: Nominal Ledger
Page: 1

Date From: 31/07/2016
Date To: 31/07/2016
N/C From:
N/C To: 99999999

Transaction From: 1
Transaction To: 99,999,999
Dept From: 0
Dept To: 999

checking corrections and adjustments

Sage does not automatically generate a report as a result of corrections to transaction data, so to confirm that the adjustments have been made, the Transactions screen or the audit trail should be checked.

The way in which a correction is reported depends on how important the change is in accounting terms. Some changes result in a simple substitution, such as a change to Details or Reference (as in the change of reference number in the Case Study). Some result in the original transaction being amended and an additional entry being inserted on the audit trail showing what has been deleted, eg where a major alteration like a change to the nominal code has been made. For example, in the audit trail extract below, transaction 83 shows the amended transaction while 84 shows the deleted transaction. The purchase of a workbench as a non-current asset – code 0020, Plant and Machinery – had been wrongly coded 5000, Materials Purchased.

Date: Time:
Tapper Timber
Audit Trail (Summary)
Page: 1

Date From: 15/08/2016
Date To: 15/08/2016
Customer From:
Customer To: ZZZZZZZZ

Transaction From: 1
Transaction To: 99,999,999
Supplier From:
Supplier To: ZZZZZZZZ

Dept From: 0
Dept To: 999
N/C From:
N/C To: 99999999

Exclude Deleted Tran: No

No	Type	Date	A/C	N/C	Dept	Ref	Details	Net	Tax	T/C	Pd	Paid	V	B	Bank Rec. Date
83	PI	15/08/2016	ET002	0020	0	9352	Workbench	500.00	100.00	T1	N	0.00	N	-	
84	PI	15/08/2016	ET002	5000	0	9352	Deleted - see tran 83	500.00	100.00	T1	N	0.00	-	-	

Changes to previous Journal transactions require a different treatment as they cannot be changed in EDIT. The way to do this is to choose the 'Journal reversals' option from the NOMINAL CODES toolbar. This will enable you to reverse (cancel out) the original journal transaction and to then enter the correct journal debit and credit entries.

Chapter Summary	■ Errors inevitably occur when processing accounts on the computer. Errors can involve incorrect references or descriptions, incorrect prices, wrong VAT codes and wrong accounts used.
	■ Most errors within Sage can be corrected using the EDIT routine within TRANSACTIONS. This will enable corrections to be made to invoices, credit notes and payments.
	■ A transaction may be deleted in full if necessary.
	■ Adjustments to Ledger accounts can also be carried out by transfers through the JOURNAL ENTRY function. This process requires a knowledge of double-entry bookkeeping.
	■ The computer accounting records may also be adjusted for situations such as account write offs and returned customer cheques.

Key Terms	**journal**	the part of the accounting system which enables you to make transfers from one General ledger account to another, and to enter new balances
	double-entry	the system of bookkeeping which involves each transaction having two entries made – a debit and a credit; computer accounting programs (which are largely single entry systems) deal with the double entry automatically
	write off	the removal of Customer (or Supplier) account transactions from the accounting records
	irrecoverable debt	a debt that is never likely to be paid and so will need to be written off. Also known as a bad debt
	returned cheque	a cheque that has been paid into a bank account but has been returned unpaid by the bank either because of lack of funds, or because of some technical irregularity on the cheque

Activities

11.1 What method of adjustment in a Sage computer accounting program would you use if:

    (a) A customer's cheque which you have paid in is returned to you marked 'cheque stopped by order of drawer'.

    (b) You discover that a payment for advertising has been input in error to the stationery account.

    (c) You are told that a credit customer who owes you money has been declared bankrupt. The debt will not be paid.

TAPPER TIMBER INPUTTING TASKS

Ensure the program date is set at 31 July 2016.

Task 1
Correct the Estate Timber Supplier invoice reference number in the Case Study on page 177 using EDIT in TRANSACTIONS.

Task 2
Carry out the Journal entries for the misposting in the Case Study on page 178. Use Ref JUL15.

Task 3
When you have completed your corrections, print out a trial balance for 31 July 2016. Check the figures on the trial balance with the figures on page 194. What has changed since the Trial Balance produced at the end of Chapter 9 and reproduced on page 191?

Sage printout checklist

The Sage printouts that follow are provided so that tutors and students carrying out the processing exercises and extended activities can periodically check their progress.

The page numbers for the relevant printouts can be found by referring to the index below.

Please note that all these printouts are © 2016 Sage (UK) Limited. All rights reserved.

book chapters

Chapter 3

Task 3

Date:			**Tapper Timber**							**Page:** 1		
Time:			**Day Books: Customer Invoices (Detailed)**									

Date From:	01/01/1980				Customer From:	
Date To:	31/12/2019				Customer To:	ZZZZZZZZ
Transaction From:	1				N/C From:	
Transaction To:	99,999,999				N/C To:	99999999
Dept From:	0					
Dept To:	999					

Tran No.	Type	Date	A/C Ref	N/C	Inv Ref	Dept.	Details	Net Amount	Tax Amount	T/C	Gross Amount	V	B
1	SI	10/06/2016	OC001	9998	10013	0	Opening Balance	2,904.20	0.00	T9	2,904.20	-	-
2	SI	17/06/2016	VH001	9998	10016	0	Opening Balance	9,900.78	0.00	T9	9,900.78	-	-
3	SI	24/06/2016	CS001	9998	10019	0	Opening Balance	5,726.88	0.00	T9	5,726.88	-	-
							Totals:	18,531.86	0.00		18,531.86		

Task 4

Date:		**Tapper Timber**		**Page:** 1
Time:		**Day Books: Supplier Invoices (Detailed)**		

Date From:	01/01/1980				Supplier From:	
Date To:	31/12/2019				Supplier To:	ZZZZZZZZ
Transaction From:	1				N/C From:	
Transaction To:	99,999,999				N/C To:	99999999
Dept From:	0					
Dept To:	999					

Tran No.	Type	Date	A/C Ref	N/C	Inv Ref	Dept	Details	Net Amount	Tax Amount	T/C	Gross Amount	V	B
4	PI	20/06/2016	CP001	9998	7611	0	Opening Balance	6,242.52	0.00	T9	6,242.52	-	-
5	PI	23/06/2016	ET001	9998	16-2408	0	Opening Balance	4,506.00	0.00	T9	4,506.00	-	-
6	PI	27/06/2016	JF001	9998	M41997	0	Opening Balance	5,006.82	0.00	T9	5,006.82	-	-
							Totals	15,755.34	0.00		15,755.34		

Task 5

Date:	**Tapper Timber**		**Page:** 1
Time:	**Period Trial Balance**		

To Period: Month 1, July 2016

N/C	Name	Debit	Credit
1100	Debtors Control Account	18,531.86	
2100	Creditors Control Account		15,755.34
9998	Suspense Account		2,776.52
	Totals:	18,531.86	18,531.86

Chapter 4

Task 3

N/C	Name	Debit	Credit

Date:
Time:

Tapper Timber
Period Trial Balance

Page: 1

To Period: Month 1, July 2016

N/C	Name	Debit	Credit
0020	Plant and Machinery	15,490.00	
0030	Office Equipment	10,965.00	
1001	Stock	18,467.18	
1100	Debtors Control Account	18,531.86	
1200	Bank Current Account	13,210.58	
1230	Petty Cash	34.68	
2100	Creditors Control Account		15,755.34
2200	Sales Tax Control Account		12,710.26
2201	Purchase Tax Control Account	8,070.10	
2300	Loans		31,303.80
3000	Capital		25,000.00
	Totals:	84,769.40	84,769.40

Chapter 5

Task 3

Date:
Time:

Tapper Timber
Day Books: Customer Invoices (Detailed)

Page: 1

| Date From: | 11/07/2016 | | | | | | Customer From: | | |
| Date To: | 14/07/2016 | | | | | | Customer To: | ZZZZZZZZ | |

Transaction From: 1   N/C From:
Transaction To: 99,999,999   N/C To: 99999999

Dept From: 0
Dept To: 999

Tran No.	Type	Date	A/C Ref	N/C	Inv Ref	Dept.	Details	Net Amount	Tax Amount	T/C	Gross Amount	V	B
30	SI	11/07/2016	CS001	4000	10026	0	Palisade fencing	2,028.00	405.60	T1	2,433.60	N	-
31	SI	12/07/2016	OC001	4000	10027	0	5-bar gates	425.00	85.00	T1	510.00	N	-
32	SI	14/07/2016	VH001	4003	10028	0	Kennels	1,138.60	227.72	T1	1,366.32	N	-
							Totals:	3,591.60	718.32		4,309.92		

Task 4

Date:						**Tapper Timber**							Page:	1
Time:						**Day Books: Customer Credits (Detailed)**								

Date From:	15/07/2016							**Customer From:**			
Date To:	15/07/2016							**Customer To:**	ZZZZZZZZ		
Transaction From:	1							**N/C From:**			
Transaction To:	99,999,999							**N/C To:**	99999999		
Dept From:	0										
Dept To:	999										

Tran No.	Type	Date	A/C Ref	N/C	Inv Ref	Dept.	Details	Net Amount	Tax Amount	T/C	Gross Amount	V	B
33	SC	15/07/2016	CS001	4002	553	0	Overcharged tack shed	140.00	28.00	T1	168.00	N	-
							Totals:	140.00	28.00		168.00		

Task 4

Date:	**Tapper Timber**	Page: 1
Time:	**Period Trial Balance**	

To Period: Month 1, July 2016

N/C	Name	Debit	Credit
0020	Plant and Machinery	15,490.00	
0030	Office Equipment	10,965.00	
1001	Stock	18,467.18	
1100	Debtors Control Account	32,833.70	
1200	Bank Current Account	13,210.58	
1230	Petty Cash	34.68	
2100	Creditors Control Account		15,755.34
2200	Sales Tax Control Account		15,093.90
2201	Purchase Tax Control Account	8,070.10	
2300	Loans		31,303.80
3000	Capital		25,000.00
4000	Sales - Fencing		2,979.60
4001	Sales - Garden furniture		2,200.00
4002	Sales - Sheds		5,600.00
4003	Sales - Animal housing		1,138.60
	Totals:	99,071.24	99,071.24

Chapter 6

Task 3

Date:		**Tapper Timber**	**Page:** 1
Time:		**Period Trial Balance**	

To Period: Month 1, July 2016

N/C	Name	Debit	Credit
0020	Plant and Machinery	17,490.00	
0030	Office Equipment	10,965.00	
1001	Stock	18,467.18	
1100	Debtors Control Account	32,833.70	
1200	Bank Current Account	13,210.58	
1230	Petty Cash	34.68	
2100	Creditors Control Account		21,526.80
2200	Sales Tax Control Account		15,093.90
2201	Purchase Tax Control Account	9,032.01	
2300	Loans		31,303.80
3000	Capital		25,000.00
4000	Sales - Fencing		2,979.60
4001	Sales - Garden furniture		2,200.00
4002	Sales - Sheds		5,600.00
4003	Sales - Animal housing		1,138.60
5000	Materials Purchased	2,809.55	
	Totals:	104,842.70	104,842.70

Chapter 7

Task 4(a)

			Tapper Timber									Page: 1

Date:
Time:

Tapper Timber

Day Books: Customer Receipts (Detailed)

Date From:	08/07/2016						Bank From:	1200
Date To:	31/07/2016						Bank To:	1200

Transaction From:	1				Customer From:	
Transaction To:	99,999,999				Customer To:	ZZZZZZZZ

Bank: 1200   **Currency:** Pound Sterling

No	Type	A/C	Date	Ref	Details	Net £	Tax £	T/C	Gross £	V	B	Bank Rec. Date
40	SR	OC001	08/07/2016 FP receipt		Sales Receipt	2,904.20	0.00	T9	2,904.20	-	N	
		-	08/07/2016	10013	2904.20 to SI 1							
41	SR	VH001	15/07/2016 Cheque		Sales Receipt	9,900.78	0.00	T9	9,900.78	-	N	
		-	15/07/2016	10016	9900.78 to SI 2							
42	SR	CS001	22/07/2016 FP receipt		Sales Receipt	5,000.00	0.00	T9	5,000.00	-	N	
		-	22/07/2016	10019	5000.00 to SI 3							
46	SR	OC001	31/07/2016 FP receipt		Sales Receipt	1,141.92	0.00	T9	1,141.92	-	N	
		-	31/07/2016	10024	631.92 to SI 26							
		-	31/07/2016	10027	510.00 to SI 31							
47	SA	OC001	31/07/2016 FP receipt		Payment on Account	358.08	0.00	T9	358.08	-	N	
48	SR	VH001	31/07/2016 Cheque		Sales Receipt	2,640.00	0.00	T9	2,640.00	-	N	
		-	31/07/2016	10023	2640.00 to SI 25							
					Totals £	**21,944.98**	**0.00**		**21,944.98**			

Task 4(b)

Date:
Time:

Tapper Timber

Day Books: Supplier Payments (Detailed)

Page: 1

Date From:	18/07/2016						Bank From:	1200
DateTo:	26/07/2016						Bank To:	1200

Transaction From:	1				Supplier From:	
Transaction To:	99,999,999				Supplier To:	ZZZZZZZZ

Bank 1200   **Currency** Pound Sterling

No	Type	A/C	Date	Ref	Details	Net £	Tax £	T/C	Gross £	V	B	Bank Rec Date
43	PP	CP001	18/07/2016 Faster		Purchase Payment	5,972.52	0.00	T9	5,972.52	-	N	
		-	18/07/2016	7611	5972.52 to PI 4							
44	PP	ET001	22/07/2016 Faster		Purchase Payment	4,506.00	0.00	T9	4,506.00	-	N	
		-	22/07/2016	16-2408	4506.00 to PI 5							
45	PP	JF001	26/07/2016 Faster		Purchase Payment	4,843.62	0.00	T9	4,843.62	-	N	
		-	26/07/2016	M41997	4843.62 to PI 6							
					Totals £	**15,322.14**	**0.00**		**15,322.14**			

Task 4(c)

Date:	**Tapper Timber**		**Page:** 1
Time:	**Period Trial Balance**		

To Period: Month 1, July 2016

N/C	Name	Debit	Credit
0020	Plant and Machinery	17,490.00	
0030	Office Equipment	10,965.00	
1001	Stock	18,467.18	
1100	Debtors Control Account	10,888.72	
1200	Bank Current Account	19,833.42	
1230	Petty Cash	34.68	
2100	Creditors Control Account		6,204.66
2200	Sales Tax Control Account		15,093.90
2201	Purchase Tax Control Account	9,032.01	
2300	Loans		31,303.80
3000	Capital		25,000.00
4000	Sales - Fencing		2,979.60
4001	Sales - Garden furniture		2,200.00
4002	Sales - Sheds		5,600.00
4003	Sales - Animal housing		1,138.60
5000	Materials Purchased	2,809.55	
	Totals:	89,520.56	89,520.56

Chapter 8

Task 1

Date:	**Tapper Timber**		**Page:** 1
Time:	**Day Books: Bank Receipts (Detailed)**		

Date From:	04/07/2016	**Bank From:**	1200
Date To:	11/07/2016	**Bank To:**	1200
Transaction From:	1	**N/C From:**	
Transaction To:	99,999,999	**N/C To:**	99999999
Dept From:	0		
Dept To:	999		

Bank: 1200   **Currency:** Pound Sterling

No	Type	N/C	Date	Ref	Details	Dept	Net £	Tax £	T/C	Gross £	V	B	Bank Rec. Date
49	BR	4001	04/07/2016	10736	Garden furniture	0	4,680.55	936.11	T1	5,616.66	N	N	
50	BR	4003	04/07/2016	10737	Animal housing	0	3,251.00	650.20	T1	3,901.20	N	N	
54	BR	4000	11/07/2016	10738	Fencing cash sales	0	865.70	173.14	T1	1,038.84	N	N	
55	BR	4002	11/07/2016	10739	Sheds cash sales	0	5,660.50	1,132.10	T1	6,792.60	N	N	
					Totals £		14,457.75	2,891.55		17,349.30			

Task 2

					Tapper Timber									Page: 1

Tapper Timber
Day Books: Bank Payments (Detailed)

Date From:	01/07/2016							Bank From:	1200
Date To:	18/07/2016							Bank To:	1200
Transaction From:	1							N/C From:	
Transaction To:	99,999,999							N/C To:	99999999
Dept From:	0								
Dept To:	999								

Bank: 1200   **Currency:** Pound Sterling

No	Type	N/C	Date	Ref	Details	Dept	Net £	Tax £	T/C	Gross £	V	B	Bank Rec. Date
51	BP	5000	01/07/2016	122992	Materials	0	1,529.60	305.92	T1	1,835.52	N	N	
52	BP	6201	07/07/2016	Debit card	Advertising	0	900.00	180.00	T1	1,080.00	N	N	
53	BP	3050	08/07/2016	Faster	Drawings	0	2,000.00	0.00	T9	2,000.00	-	N	
56	BP	7550	13/07/2016	Faster	Telephone bill	0	312.00	62.40	T1	374.40	N	N	
57	BP	7700	18/07/2016	Debit card	Equipment hire	0	456.00	91.20	T1	547.20	N	N	
					Totals £		5,197.60	639.52		5,837.12			

Task 4

Tapper Timber
Period Trial Balance

Page: 1

To Period: Month 1, July 2016

N/C	Name	Debit	Credit
0020	Plant and Machinery	17,490.00	
0030	Office Equipment	10,965.00	
0050	Motor Vehicles	17,995.00	
1001	Stock	18,467.18	
1100	Debtors Control Account	10,888.72	
1200	Bank Current Account	14,751.60	
1230	Petty Cash	34.68	
2100	Creditors Control Account		6,204.66
2200	Sales Tax Control Account		17,985.45
2201	Purchase Tax Control Account	13,270.53	
2300	Loans		31,303.80
3000	Capital		30,000.00
3050	Drawings	2,000.00	
4000	Sales - Fencing		3,845.30
4001	Sales - Garden furniture		6,880.55
4002	Sales - Sheds		11,260.50
4003	Sales - Animal housing		4,389.60
5000	Materials Purchased	4,339.15	
6201	Advertising	900.00	
7550	Telephone and Fax	312.00	
7700	Equipment Hire	456.00	
	Totals:	111,869.86	111,869.86

Chapter 9

Task 2

												Bank Rec.
Date:					**Tapper Timber**						**Page:** 1	
Time:				**Day Books: Cash Payments (Detailed)**								

Date From: 07/07/2016 **Bank From:** 1230
Date To: 28/07/2016 **Bank To:** 1230

Transaction From: 1 **N/C From:**
Transaction To: 99,999,999 **N/C To:** 99999999

Dept From: 0
Dept To: 999

Bank: 1230 **Currency:** Pound Sterling

No	Type	N/C	Date	Ref	Details	Dept	Net £	Tax £	T/C	Gross £	V	B	Bank Rec. Date
62	CP	7801	07/07/2016	PC101	Cleaning materials	0	36.00	7.20	T1	43.20	N	-	
63	CP	7501	14/07/2016	PC102	Postage stamps	0	25.00	0.00	T2	25.00	N	-	
64	CP	7502	20/07/2016	PC103	Envelopes	0	16.00	3.20	T1	19.20	N	-	
67	CP	5003	28/07/2016	PC106	Packaging	0	4.00	0.80	T1	4.80	N	-	
					Totals £		81.00	11.20		92.20			

Date: **Tapper Timber** **Page:** 1
Time: **Day Books: Cash Receipts (Detailed)**

Date From: 25/07/2016 **Bank From:** 1230
Date To: 28/07/2016 **Bank To:** 1230

Transaction From: 1 **N/C From:**
Transaction To: 99,999,999 **N/C To:** 99999999

Dept From: 0
Dept To: 999

Bank: 1230 **Currency:** Pound Sterling

No	Type	N/C	Date	Ref	Details	Dept	Net £	Tax £	T/C	Gross £	V	B	Bank Rec. Date
65	CR	7502	25/07/2016	PC104	A4 paper sold to	0	3.00	0.60	T1	3.60	N	-	
66	CR	7501	28/07/2016	PC105	Postage stamps	0	3.15	0.00	T2	3.15	N	-	
					Totals £		6.15	0.60		6.75			

Task 3(a)

Date: 14/01/2016 **Tapper Timber** **Page:** 1
Time: 10:40:06 **Day Books: Bank Receipts (Detailed)**

Date From: 15/07/2016 **Bank From:** 1235
Date To: 22/07/2016 **Bank To:** 1235

Transaction From: 1 **N/C From:**
Transaction To: 99,999,999 **N/C To:** 99999999

Dept From: 0
Dept To: 999

Bank: 1235 **Currency:** Pound Sterling

No	Type	N/C	Date	Ref	Details	Dept	Net £	Tax £	T/C	Gross £	V	B	Bank Rec. Date
68	BR	4002	15/07/2016	T001	Sheds cash sales	0	3,015.85	603.17	T1	3,619.02	N	-	
69	BR	4000	15/07/2016	T002	Fencing cash sales	0	1,463.40	292.68	T1	1,756.08	N	-	
70	BR	4003	22/07/2016	T003	Animal housing	0	604.00	120.80	T1	724.80	N	-	
71	BR	4001	22/07/2016	T004	Garden furniture	0	5,921.05	1,184.21	T1	7,105.26	N	-	
					Totals £		11,004.30	2,200.86		13,205.16			

Task 5

			Page: 1
Date: **Time:**	**Tapper Timber** **Period Trial Balance**		

To Period: Month 1, July 2016

N/C	Name	Debit	Credit
0020	Plant and Machinery	17,490.00	
0030	Office Equipment	10,965.00	
0050	Motor Vehicles	17,995.00	
1001	Stock	18,467.18	
1100	Debtors Control Account	10,888.72	
1200	Bank Current Account	27,501.76	
1230	Petty Cash	49.23	
2100	Creditors Control Account		6,204.66
2200	Sales Tax Control Account		20,186.91
2201	Purchase Tax Control Account	13,301.73	
2300	Loans		31,303.80
3000	Capital		30,000.00
3050	Drawings	2,000.00	
4000	Sales - Fencing		5,308.70
4001	Sales - Garden furniture		12,801.60
4002	Sales - Sheds		14,276.35
4003	Sales - Animal housing		4,993.60
4904	Rent Income		200.00
5000	Materials Purchased	4,339.15	
5003	Packaging	4.00	
6201	Advertising	900.00	
7103	General Rates	350.00	
7104	Premises Insurance	85.00	
7501	Postage and Carriage	21.85	
7502	Office Stationery	13.00	
7550	Telephone and Fax	312.00	
7700	Equipment Hire	456.00	
7801	Cleaning	136.00	
	Totals:	125,275.62	125,275.62

Chapter 10

Task 1

Date: Time:				Tapper Timber Nominal Activity							Page:	1	
Date From: Date To:	01/07/2016 31/07/2016								N/C From: N/C To:	4000 4000			
Transaction From: Transaction To:	1 99,999,999												

| N/C: | 4000 | | Name: | Fencing | | | | | Account Balance: | | 5,308.70 CR | |

No	Type	Date	Account	Ref	Details	Dept	T/C	Value	Debit	Credit	V	B
26	SI	05/07/2016	OC001	10024	Stock fencing	0	T1	658.25		658.25	N	-
29	SC	07/07/2016	OC001	552	Stock fencing damaged	0	T1	131.65	131.65		N	-
30	SI	11/07/2016	CS001	10026	Palisade fencing	0	T1	2,028.00		2,028.00	N	-
31	SI	12/07/2016	OC001	10027	5-bar gates	0	T1	425.00		425.00	N	-
54	BR	11/07/2016	1200	10738	Fencing cash sales	0	T1	865.70		865.70	N	N
69	BR	15/07/2016	1235	T002	Fencing cash sales	0	T1	1,463.40		1,463.40	N	-
							Totals:		131.65	5,440.35		
							History Balance:			5,308.70		

Task 3

Date: Time:				Tapper Timber Audit Trail (Detailed)							Page:	1
Date From: Date To:	31/07/2016 31/07/2016								Customer From: Customer To:		ZZZZZZZZ	
Transaction From: Transaction To:	1 99,999,999								Supplier From: Supplier To:		ZZZZZZZZ	
Exclude Deleted	No											

No	Type	A/C	N/C	Dp	Details	Date	Ref	Net	Tax	T/C	Pd	Paid	V	B	Bank Rec. Date
46	SR	OC001				31/07/2016	FP receipt	1,141.92	0.00		Y	1,141.92	R		31/07/2016
		46	1200	0	Sales Receipt			1,141.92	0.00	T9		1,141.92	-		
					631.92 to SI 26	31/07/2016	10024					631.92			
					510.00 to SI 31	31/07/2016	10027					510.00			
47	SA	OC001				31/07/2016	FP receipt	358.08	0.00		N	0.00	R		31/07/2016
		47	1200	0	Payment on Account			358.08	0.00	T9		0.00	-		
48	SR	VH001				31/07/2016	Cheque	2,640.00	0.00		Y	2,640.00	N		
		48	1200	0	Sales Receipt			2,640.00	0.00	T9		2,640.00			
					2640.00 to SI 25	31/07/2016	10023					2,640.00			
80	BP	1200				31/07/2016	Bank	50.00	0.00		Y	50.00	R		31/07/2016
		80	7901	0	Bank charges			50.00	0.00	T2		50.00	N		

Task 4

Back up   ✕

Back up company
Advanced options
Previous backups

Company details

You are about to create a backup of:

Company name: Tapper Timber

Found in: C:\PROGRAMDATA\SAGE\ACCOUNTS\2016\COMPANY.000\

Where do you want the company backed up to?

To select a location to save this backup to, click Browse. We have suggested a filename for this backup. If you are happy with this suggestion, click OK.

Backing up to removable media? Insert the device before clicking OK.

The Backup manager can back up your data automatically. For more information, press F1.

Filename*: | Chapter 11 end

Location*: | F:\

[Browse...]

Note: Your filename and location may be different.

[OK]   [Cancel]   [Help]

Chapter 11

Task 3

Date: Time:		**Tapper Timber** **Period Trial Balance**		Page:　1

To Period:　　Month 1, July 2016

N/C	Name	Debit	Credit
0020	Plant and Machinery	17,490.00	
0030	Office Equipment	10,965.00	
0050	Motor Vehicles	17,995.00	
1001	Stock	18,467.18	
1100	Debtors Control Account	10,888.72	
1200	Bank Current Account	27,451.76	
1230	Petty Cash	49.23	
2100	Creditors Control Account		6,204.66
2200	Sales Tax Control Account		20,186.91
2201	Purchase Tax Control Account	13,301.73	
2300	Loans		31,303.80
3000	Capital		30,000.00
3050	Drawings	2,000.00	
4000	Sales - Fencing		5,308.70
4001	Sales - Garden furniture		12,801.60
4002	Sales - Sheds		13,076.35
4003	Sales - Animal housing		6,193.60
4904	Rent Income		200.00
5000	Materials Purchased	4,339.15	
5003	Packaging	4.00	
6201	Advertising	900.00	
7103	General Rates	350.00	
7104	Premises Insurance	85.00	
7501	Postage and Carriage	21.85	
7502	Office Stationery	13.00	
7550	Telephone and Fax	312.00	
7700	Equipment Hire	456.00	
7801	Cleaning	136.00	
7901	Bank Charges	50.00	
	Totals:	125,275.62	125,275.62

Bank Current Account balance reduced by £50 (bank charges)

Bank Charges amount added (£50)

Sales - Sheds reduced by £1200

Sales - Animal housing increased by £1,200

Answers to chapter activities

CHAPTER 1: INTRODUCTION TO USING ACCOUNTING SOFTWARE

1.1   Passwords, which should not be revealed to unauthorised parties, enable access to computer systems and to specific programs, eg computer accounting packages. Access rights operate within software packages and restrict employees to certain types of transaction. Computer accounting packages normally contain very sensitive information, eg details of customers (how much they owe and how good they are at paying), payroll (how much employees earn), all of which needs to be protected against unauthorised access. Passwords protect the data from outsiders and unauthorised employees; access rights further protect sensitive data from employees.

1.2   The system date is the date that the computer thinks the date is. It will normally be allocated to any transaction carried out or file created on that date. The program date is different from the system date. It can be allocated to a set of transactions, eg a series of cheques paid into the bank last week which you want to carry that date from the previous week. In short: system date = actual date, program date = date you are allocating.

1.3   Back-up disks could include: a set locked up on the premises at the close of business each day, a set taken home by an employee at the close of business each day.

1.4   You should carry out a 'restore' routine from the latest set of back-up disks. This will unfortunately mean that you will have to re-input the transactions since the last back-up, but it is better than losing the whole lot.

1.5   Install anti-virus software which will create a firewall to protect your system against virus invasion. Update the software regularly. Warn employees against opening up 'spam' emails with attachments which might contain viruses.

CHAPTER 2: SETTING UP THE BUSINESS

2.1   Wizards, computer manual, on-screen Help.

2.2   Company details, financial year, VAT details, passwords and access rights.

2.3   **(a)**   Customers

      (b)   Suppliers

      (c)   Nominal

CHAPTER 3: SETTING UP RECORDS FOR CUSTOMERS AND SUPPLIERS

3.1   False.

3.2   **(a)**   A customer who has bought on credit and who owes money

      (b)   A supplier who supplies on credit and who is owed money

3.3   **(a)**   Sales Ledger

      (b)   Purchases Ledger

3.4 **(a)** The total amount owed by receivables (debtors) – ie customers

(b) The total amount owing to payables (creditors) – ie suppliers

3.5 A trade discount is an agreed percentage reduction in the selling price of goods or services given to regular customers.

A settlement (or 'cash') discount is an agreed percentage reduction in the selling price of goods or services given when early payment is made within a specified time period.

3.6 Trial balance.

3.7 Account reference – needed for input into the accounting system.

Credit limit – needed to ensure that the level of credit given to the customer can be monitored and controlled.

3.8 Only if there are no transactions on it.

CHAPTER 4: SETTING UP THE GENERAL LEDGER

4.1 A list of accounts, classified into various function areas, covering the accounting needs of a business.

4.2

Categories	Description
Sales	income from the sale of goods or services – accounts can be allocated for different types of sales
Purchases	items bought to produce goods to sell – accounts can be allocated for different types of purchases
Direct expenses	expenses incurred which are directly related to producing the goods
Overheads	expenses which have to be paid and which are not directly related to producing the goods
Fixed assets	items which are bought to keep in the business in the long term
Current assets	items owned, or owed to, the business in the short term
Current liabilities	items owed by the business in the short term
Long-term liabilities	items owed by the business in the long term
Capital & reserves	the financial investment of the owner(s) of the business

4.3
(a) &
(b)

Account name	Account number	Category
Freehold Property	0010	fixed assets
Office Equipment	0030	fixed assets
Motor Vehicles	0050	fixed assets
Materials Purchased	5000	purchases
Bank Current Account	1200	current assets
Creditors Control	2100	current liabilities
Directors Salaries	7001	overheads
Electricity	7200	overheads
Capital	3000	capital & reserves

CHAPTER 5: SELLING TO CUSTOMERS ON CREDIT

5.1 Purchase order, delivery note, invoice, credit note, statement, remittance advice.

5.2 False.

5.3 False.

5.4 The two most important are the amount to be paid and when it has to be paid.

5.5 Customers who have bought on credit from the business.

5.6 Sales Ledger.

5.7 The batch totals should be checked against the invoice or credit note totals calculated by the computer from the input.

5.8 Customer account number, date, invoice number, details of invoice, net amount and tax code.

5.9 The tax code input automatically calculates the amount of VAT due on the invoice goods total. The VAT value is posted to the Sales Tax Control Account.

CHAPTER 6: BUYING FROM SUPPLIERS ON CREDIT

6.1 Suppliers who supply on credit and who are owed money.

6.2 Purchases Ledger ('Suppliers' in Sage). This shows how much is owed to each supplier.

6.3 Purchases relate to materials or items bought to produce or provide the actual product of the business; expenses are running costs incurred (note that these are not the same as 'direct expenses' in the Chart of Accounts); capital items are items bought for long-term use in the business. It is important to identify each of these types so that the correct account number (and therefore Chart of Accounts category) can be allocated.

6.4 See text on page 89 for input procedure. Note the importance of checking the VAT on-screen.

The invoices should be checked for irregularities before input and any problems identified and dealt with.

After input the batch total should be checked against the computer total – a Day Book Report could be printed to provide this figure.

CHAPTER 7: CUSTOMER AND SUPPLIER PAYMENTS

7.1 Bank payment = cash (ie non-credit) payment to a supplier

Supplier payment = payment to a supplier who has sold on credit terms

Bank receipt = cash (ie non-credit) payment from a customer

Customer receipt = payment from a customer who has bought on credit

7.2 If no remittance advice is received the business will not know – until the bank statement arrives – that the payment has been received. The remittance advice also provides input details (amount, date, references and allocation details) for the business.

7.3 Payment from a credit customer – accounting entries are: a debit to the bank account, which will increase, and a credit to the customer account, which will decrease (owe less).

Payment to supplier (assuming credit is given) – accounting entries are: a credit to the bank account, which will decrease, and a debit to the supplier account, which will decrease (the business will owe less).

7.4 A Supplier Payments Day Book Report will show the total of payments made to suppliers in any given date range.

CHAPTER 8: CASH RECEIPTS AND PAYMENTS

8.1 Bank receipt.

8.2 Bank payment.

8.3 **(a)** £120.00 to Bank Account, £100.00 to Sales Account, £20.00 to Sales VAT Account.

(b) £160.00 to Purchases VAT Account, £960.00 to Bank Account, £800.00 to Purchases Account.

8.4 Examples include: capital invested by the owner, loans, grants, rent received.

CHAPTER 9: BANK ACCOUNTS, PETTY CASH AND RECURRING ENTRIES

9.1 **(a)** Transfers in: Transfer screen from Bank Accounts, transfer from Bank Current Account 1200 to Petty Cash account 1230.

(b) Payments out: Bank Payment screen from Bank Accounts, payment from Petty Cash account 1230 coded with appropriate Nominal code.

(c) Receipts in: Bank receipt screen from Bank Accounts, receipt in Petty Cash account 1230 coded with appropriate Nominal code.

9.2 **(a)** There is no VAT on stamps – code T2 (VAT exempt) should be used.

(b) There is VAT on stationery at standard rate (T1). The VAT can be calculated either manually, or by using the 'Calc Net' button at the top of the screen.

(c) The voucher should be referred to a higher authority; it cannot be processed if the transaction is unauthorised.

9.3 **(a)** Daily takings should be entered as Bank Receipts. Record payments into the bank account as a Transfer from Cash Register Account to Bank Current Account, using the paying-in slip as the source document.

(b) Security risk. The money could be better employed on the bank account, paying bills etc.

9.4 Recurring entries are normally for regular bank receipts and payments. Receipts include items such as rent received and payments include items such as rates, loan repayments and insurance premiums.

CHAPTER 10: REPORTS AND ROUTINES

10.1 To monitor and maintain the accuracy of the double-entry bookkeeping system: the two columns should always agree.

10.2 A computer accounting system is a single entry system: a debit always generates an equal credit (or credits) and vice versa and so the total of debits and credits will always automatically be the same.

10.3 A trial balance provides management with useful information such as the balance of the bank account, the level of sales and individual expenses of the business.

10.4 Order of input.

10.5 **(a)** An Aged Debtors Analysis shows the amounts that individual customers owe and how long the debt has been outstanding. It enables management to identify the customers that need to be chased up and any bad debts that may have to be written off.

(b) An Aged Creditor Analysis shows the amounts that are owing to individual suppliers and how long each debt has been outstanding. It enables the business to schedule payments to suppliers and make the most of credit granted.

10.6 **(a)** £10,888.72

(b) Debtors Control Account

(c) The account is in arrears (assuming a 30 day credit period). A customer statement.

10.7 **(a)** £27,501.76

(b) Petty cash £49.23

(c) Total sales = £37,380.25

CHAPTER 11: CORRECTIONS AND ADJUSTMENTS

11.1 **(a)** Write off, Refunds and Returns Wizard – Customer Cheque Returns function.

(b) Journal entry (debit Advertising Account, credit Stationery Account).

(c) Write off, Refunds and Returns Wizard – Write off Customer Accounts.

Index

for your notes

for your notes